"*RABBIT WARRIOR* reflects
want to put it down. I felt a:
ten with courage, integrity and perseverance.

MW00626404

SHEILA MURPHY, author and *Cardinal House* poet, directs memoir
and poetry workshops at Wesleyan University's Institute for
Lifelong Learning in Middletown, Connecticut.

"JANET CALHOUN'S courageous vulnerability in this book is
stunning. As she seeks healing from personal loss and inner pain, she
turns to other writers for help and inward into herself. Her beloved
Cape Cod provides the refuge she needs, and it is there that she
observes, questions, probes, and relentlessly seeks peace and closure.
She submits to the journey and creates a rhythm between the pain of
the past and the beauty and solitude of the present. Finding parallels
in nature, she allows it to instruct her with its lessons about vulnerability, protections, following instincts, and accepting outcomes.
Read this book and you'll be talking to the animals, too. And you'll
be asking yourself a lot of questions. Calhoun inspires us to face our
own pain and grief with the determination to heal."

DOLORES PARSIL, author of
Lancaster's Good Man, John Piersol McCaskey

"AS A FELLOW MEMOIRIST, I admire Calhoun's willingness to
go to those sometimes painful places in our lives and emerge with a
renewed spirit about life. Already, *Rabbit Warrior* has enabled this
reader to move on with her life and achieve happiness. This memoir
has had a profound influence on me. Thank you, Janet, for going to
those places before me and searching for truth . . . it really does set us
free. The 'rabbit' hops throughout the memoir, reminding us of the
journey's universal truths."

MARRA GIULIANO, memoir writer

"When I began the book I, frankly, was a little worried. My internal thoughts were something along the lines of, "oh no, here goes another person's documentation of extensive navel-gazing." I was wrong.

The success of your book is due, in part, to the commonality of the human condition. Without taking anything from the uniqueness of your family, personal history, and experiences, you nevertheless bring to light issues many of us face. Your journey to potential spiritual solutions help feed reflection and possibilities for the reader.

I am in awe of you, Phil and your daughters for allowing and being willing to, as you say, stand naked in public. That is a wonderful gift given to you by your husband and daughters. That kind of courage which benefits others is rare today. It requires those of us who read your book the obligation to deeply respect and honor the gift given by you and your family.

It is clear despite your public thanks to multiple editors that you are a gifted writer who has been honing her craft for some time. Your use of reflection coupled and interspersed with an accounting of events in your history and the description of your summer alone in the Cape kept me engaged. What is next in your writing journey?

Thanks again for inviting me into your world and that of your family. I'm "digesting" and incorporating your insights into my life."

WES FARMER, PhD

"FIVE STARS! Great Read... a poignant personal story with lessons for all. Could not put it down."

TOM C.

Janet Brady Calhoun

RABBIT
WARRIOR

A CAPE COD PILGRIMAGE
OF HEALING AND SELF-DISCOVERY

R A B B I T
W A R R I O R

by Janet Brady Calhoun

Copyright © 2016
All rights reserved.

Cover Artwork by: Ky Colestock

Library of Congress Number: 2016917113
International Standard Book Number: 978-1-60126-516-6

The author may be contacted through her blog at rabbitwarrior.com
or her email at janet@rabbitwarrior.com

Masthof Press
219 Mill Road | Morgantown, PA 19543-9516
www.Masthof.com

DEDICATED TO:

Dr. John Joseph Brady, my father, and Martel Strayer
Brady, my mother, who birthed my soul;

my husband, Phil, who always believed;

my daughters, Susan Calhoun, Tracy Calhoun Becker,
who have walked my journey with me;

and my grandchildren, Victoria and Payton Becker and
Luke Washinger, who light up my world with hope.

"Writing is enormously painful, and writing this story is sometimes excruciating. Writing each day, I go through the emotions I felt at the time of the story I'm remembering, I relive the hell. But I also relive the moments of hope and miracle and love."

David Sheff, beautiful boy

"The life of the spirit is never static. We're born on one level, only to find some new struggle toward wholeness gestating within. That's the sacred intent of life . . . to move continuously toward growth, toward recovering all that is lost and orphaned within us and restoring the divine image imprinted on our soul."

Sue Monk Kidd

TABLE OF CONTENTS

ACKNOWLEDGMENTS

I am deeply grateful to the following people who took time out of their lives to support, encourage, and believe in *Rabbit Warrior*.

Phil Calhoun, Joan Calhoun, Joyce and Marty Halpert, Susan Calhoun, Tracy Becker, Joyce LeGrande, Marra Giuliano, Paula Graham, Sheila Murphy, Marlene Arnold, fellow author Dolores Parsil, and my editor and friend, Lois Strause. And special thanks to Liz Kresge who blessed our family with her therapeutic gifts and Ky Colestock, a high school classmate and friend, whose artistic talents created the magical rabbit that graces *Rabbit Warrior's* cover.

And, a special thank you, to Masthof Press' Dan Mast and Lois Ann Mast, for their enthusiastic support of *Rabbit Warrior's* journey.

I apologize to anyone inadvertently forgotten who accompanied me on this healing journey after loss

of loved ones,

of parts of myself,

of magical thinking and myths.

INTRODUCTION

A rabbit emerged from the underbrush, cautiously searched the yard and sky for any predatory threat and then scratched a resting hollow in the grass. From time to time she glanced over her shoulder towards the underbrush, as if reassuring herself that protective cover was readily available should any threat arise.

Each of us is born with a rabbit's vulnerabilities and an innate sense that our emotional and physical survival depends upon a vigilant awareness of external threats to our well-being. Rabbits instinctively build protective nests with open-ended escape routes both front and back. Humans build protective nests by accommodating and endearing themselves to others, accumulating material possessions and seeking religious and philosophical certitude. Yet both rabbits and humans instinctively understand there are no safe places to hide.

Sometimes, when life wounds and weakens us, we don our warrior's armor around our most vulnerable places and march into battle determined to win over formidable foes. Other times, life's challenges threaten to collapse our battling spirits and we turn within.

Rabbit Warrior is about one woman's pilgrimage to mourn, heal, and confront real and imagined foes in order to live more abundantly. Years of accumulated scar tissue and layers of protective armor had prevented me from identifying my own voice.

Having lost, within a seven-month period, my mother and sister, two of the most significant women in my life, I retreated to our Cape Cod cottage for the summer where I howled myself into an exhausted silence.

Emptied out, I turned inward.

Daily journal writing exposed persons, places and memories stored deep within. Struggling to identify my authentic voice, I was challenged to unmask falsehoods, give up protective magical thinking, and examine tragically difficult moments, as well as rejoice in my many blessings. One day's writing carried me to places unimagined through glorious insights and perspectives; the next day's writing warned of painful places best avoided. I wrestled with fear, guilt and anxiety. What if my rumination irretrievably damaged the relationships that had always sustained me? Feelings of disloyalty and confusion threatened to abort my efforts. Nevertheless, I continued to be driven forward by an underlying belief that this pilgrimage would ultimately restore me to myself.

Journal writing exposed disjointed pieces of my life, and like a reassembled jigsaw puzzle, as pieces merged, larger images became clear, and my understanding of where I needed to go and how to get there gained clarity.

Nature also mentored me in powerful ways. She helped

me to understand the integral parts of life: change and evolution; pain and suffering; death and dying. Her many voices could be heard, only if first I stilled my own. As I walked the beaches and forested Cape paths, I heard nature's voices through a horseshoe crab, lobster, hummingbird . . . rabbits and a great blue heron; voices that spoke to me of tenacity, protection, survival and adaptation to life's challenges. No longer able to hear the significant voices of my mother and sister, other powerful voices began to fill the void.

Writers, soul-seekers on their own challenging journeys towards self-actualization, reached out to me, confirming the validity of my struggle. They helped me to dispel guilt, expunge destructive messages, peel away emotional layers accumulated over decades, moving ever deeper towards my core, my authentic voice. Stumbling through the dark, with fear and pain ripping at my resolve and urging me to stop, I felt these courageously honest writers reaching through the pages of their books and wrapping their arms around me.

"I'm just trying to get home.
Life is a journey to get home . . .
a circular process we search in
many places, through many people,
trying to get home."

Bob Dylan lyric

CHAPTER ONE

CAPE COD PILGRIMAGE

*L*oss reshapes the soul.

My spirit felt deadened by the recent loss of my mother and sister, two of the most significant women in my life. The space once filled by their internalized voices morphed into a black vacuous hole. Scar tissue from past losses never adequately mourned began to merge with more recent losses and filled the hole with blood-red mourning. *"Compartmentalize your losses or they will crush you. If you remain unable to identify your own voice, you will not survive. Who are you?"*

Explosive thunderheads hung in the air of my Audi wagon, thunderheads filled with bolts of unanticipated fire. It felt as if the oxygen had been sucked from my car by the approaching emotional storms, making it hard to breathe. The thunderheads' roiling darkness had been gathering for some time, but during the eight-hour drive alone, I lost the mental agility and emotional will to hold their threatening power at bay.

1

Feeling naked and alone in the direct path of the approaching emotional storms, my sixty-four-year-old soul shouted, *"Stand fast, Janet. Believe you can do this. This quixotic quest to joust with your demons and dragons and cross moats to scale impenetrable fortress walls, behind which hide many precious secrets, will ultimately set your spirit free. Stand fast."*

Leaving the bridge, I spotted the rotary's topiary shrub's Cape Cod greeting, a visual confirmation that the long driving journey from Pennsylvania was almost over. I sensed that a much more arduous journey was about to begin. I opened the Audi sunroof, filling the car with the sensuously soft Cape Cod air and felt the warm caress of the sunlight splash across my shoulders. It felt as though the sky was giving me permission to run away: to enjoy the luxury of being answerable to no one but myself.

As heavy traffic on the road connecting the rotary and Route 6A brought me to a standstill, my spirit searched for the means to emerge from this suffocating darkness into light, to understand both the journey and self more fully. *Who had I been? Who was I now? And, who might I become?* Recent therapy sessions had shaken loose my "saving rabbits syndrome," a need to nurture those I perceived as neglected and emotionally vulnerable. With my therapist, I explored my disproportionate need for approval and love, even if that meant allowing others to define me. My therapeutic summer assignment was to more deeply explore this "saving rabbits syndrome," and to outline steps needed to redefine and reclaim myself.

As the Cape traffic began to inch forward, I thought about how I had never spent any extended time alone. My husband Phil had sensed my spirit collapsing and suggested reflective time alone at our Cape house might be helpful. I felt a nauseating homesickness thrashing against the edges of my mind. *Will my family be safe while I am gone? Is this summer journey too self-indulgent, too narcissistic? What if they should need me in a hurry and I am so far away?* A caution flag emerged in my mind.

You know that whenever you are separated from, or even anticipate being separated from loved ones, homesickness overwhelms and disorients you, limiting your ability to fully explore life's opportunities. If you are going to spend the summer on the Cape with a minimum of family contact, you must confront and subdue your homesick demons. What is home exactly? Is it an exterior or an interior concept, or both?

I began to play with the notion of homesickness, thinking that if I could more clearly understand it, I might be able to control it. *Could homesickness be considered as longing for those we love who are not with us, or as unresolved relational issues that occur in the home? Could it be defined as an estrangement from our inner core? What exactly causes the gnawing emptiness that I have always carried inside? Why do I feel anxious each time I transition from Lancaster to the Cape or the Cape to Lancaster? My internal duality confuses me; on the one hand I rejoice in family, on the other hand I rejoice in the luxury of solitude. In each case I struggle to quell intermittent bouts of anxiety.*

My mother often spoke of suffering from homesickness, while at the same time laughingly asking how that was possible, since she never had a real home. At twelve, Mother's world crumbled. Her mother abandoned the family without a word, leaving Mother with a father known to be unaffectionate and unyielding in his convictions. I'm not sure I ever would have known about the abandonment if I had not been asked by my grandfather to get him a paper from the steel box he kept in the bottom of his bedroom closet.

The giant red "A" emboldened on each page of my grandparents' divorce papers blasted into my reality. My grandmother had a "Scarlet Letter" figuratively pinned to her chest like eighteenth century Hester Prynne! I felt lightheaded and disoriented. Sitting cross-legged on the bedroom floor, I was stunned that my mother had never spoken of her childhood trauma. *How did my mother's twelve-year-old soul absorb the traumatic public humiliation of adultery, along with her father's bitter male fury?* I wondered if there might be other secrets hidden in my mother's heart.

I thought of my grandmother as well, trying to make sense of the notion that twentieth century women suffered the same inhumane fate for infidelity as women did hundreds of years ago. *In my heart I can forgive you for running from a loveless marriage. I cannot forgive you for deserting your child.*

When I shared with Mother what I had found, she told me about hiding behind her bedroom curtains as she watched her mother and a hired hand kiss just inside the milk house door, while her father milked cows just steps away; she spoke of feeling enormous fear for her mother if her father found out, as well as fear for herself if what she had seen led to her mother "going off with that stranger." Fear became reality, her mother did leave for two years without saying good-bye.

"But, she returned and I welcomed her back into my life." My mother then smiled reassuringly and said, "I survived, Janet. It wasn't easy. I had the back of my feet stoned walking home from school. I was shunned. But I survived! Remember that. I'm sorry you found the papers. It was a long time ago. Let's not talk of this again." She never did. The divorce papers disappeared from my grandfather's box.

I've often thought about the turmoil and confusion my mother must have felt when abandoned at twelve. Ironically, this was the same age I was when my father died. Parental abandonment, by choice or through death, burns a hole into the spirit that never fully heals.

Mother spent a lifetime trying to control her fear of abandonment and attempting to recapture a sense of home. Her struggle became her children's struggle as well.

Could my homesickness be merely an extension of my mother's internalized parental anxieties? Or, did my forty-seven-year-old dad's traumatic death from an inoperable malignant brain tumor and the resultant destabilization in my formative years, create a permanent longing to recapture my childhood home? Or, had the traumatic loss of a loved one created fear that I would not be nearby when a loved one needed support? Or, that a loved one might die without having had a chance to say good-bye? Could my homesickness be a result of never having found myself? Could alienation from self be the source of homesickness? Is home internal?

I suspected that this complex series of questions would be followed by many more. With my spirit feeling so numb and entrapped in mourning, I would need some way to keep track of all these mental and emotional challenges. I decided that when I arrived at the Cape house, I would start a personal journal, a sort of mental template, listing issues to be addressed and capturing emerging insights.

But right then, I felt so exhausted and overwhelmed, the decision to start a journal was the only decision I could make about anything. One foot in front of the other . . . one hour . . . one day at a time. My heart fluttered, quietly resonating to the notion that I could live in my moment, listen to my rhythms and make instantaneous decisions based on what I needed. *I will follow the white rabbit down her magical transformative hole, I thought, trusting that she will lead me where I need to go. Who knows what transformative discoveries I will make. What creatures of wonder will lead me on a path of self-discovery? Hopefully, I will not be diverted by angry queens who want to "off my head."*

I drove onto the Cape's Route 6 east determined to avail myself of all the opportunities afforded by the reflective isolation at my personal Walden Pond, my Cape house . . . my cabin . . . my beloved bay—as Thoreau so beautifully put it, "to live deliberately." My family had been coming to Cape Cod each summer for thirty-five years. I knew how this place gave you permission to just be. I determined to use the solitude to revisit past relationships, deal with whatever insights those relationships provided, and make peace with the past. Then let it go to concentrate my energies on developing who I would become for the rest of my life. I pledged to banish my demons and discover my glory.

As I meandered along Route 6A, taking in the miles of historically charming cottages, detecting the sweet smell of my

Cape Cod Bay, I thought about how the "shoulds" of others had always defined my life. My mother always told me that I was beautiful, talented, and loved unconditionally. But she had also told me that I should be something more, should have made some different choices. *Unconditionally loved, but somehow inadequate. A mixed and confusing message. Could that be why I lack self-confidence even as those around me say I have it all?* Yet another question for my journal's exploratory list.

Turning off Route 6A onto the sandy road that leads to our Cape house, a poignant memory popped into my mind: as if she were lighting my way, I recalled my six year old granddaughter Victoria's reply when asked who she wanted to be when she grew up, "I'm going to be me when I grow up." At the time, I was struck by the confident wise simplicity of her reply. I pulled into the driveway, turned the car off and sat looking at the bay. As the beauty, solitude and peace of this secluded spot crept into my soul, I thought about Victoria's comment and realized that in my sixty-four years I had never really known me. Could that be because I had always permitted others to define who I was, who I should be? I had allowed externals to define me. My challenge over the next three months would be to strip away imposed externals to find my center.

As I walked past dozens of profusely blooming purple and pink hydrangea bushes surrounding the meandering brick walk leading to the front door, I passed the smiling Buddhist sculptural head sitting atop a granite Buddhist mile marker, a marker placed one mile from Tibetan monasteries to let spiritual seekers know they only had a mile to go to reach their destination. I stopped, engaged in her peaceful all-knowing smile and stroked her nose, as I ritually did every time I passed her. "Lady Buddha, I'm back," I whispered. "I have a lot longer than a mile to go. I will need your help to find the Way."

I unlocked the front door and stepped inside, standing perfectly still so I could look through the wall of glass over the abandoned cranberry bog to the bay. I felt a sense of peace and joy undulating from the bottom of my feet all the way to my heart. I could not help but smile amidst my tears.

I dropped my suitcases and canvas book bag at the foot of the stairs, determined to walk through the house, allowing its beauty and peacefulness to penetrate my being.

Honey-colored antique pine floors, oriental carpets, an imported French country table with eight wheat-sheave-backed rush seated chairs graced the room. The hand-painted French cupboard, that opens to reveal a bar with lighted glass shelves holding wine glasses with multi-colored sea creature stems, glowed with reflection from the setting sun. I thought about the laughter of good friends and family sharing food and wine around that table for years. I took in the white kitchen cupboards, the exquisitely marbled counters which held treasured pieces of sculpture and pottery collected from around the country. The kitchen opened into the dining and living room so there would be no artificial barriers between the chef and friends, and the sunroom's wood burning stove was visible from the kitchen so I could cook and dream simultaneously.

Watercolors and oil paintings splashed against the palest of yellow walls to reflect the colors of sunshine and the blue bay. As I strolled through the two first-floor guest bedrooms and bath, I thought about all the loved ones and special friends who had slept there—all the laughter and tears. I decided it was time for a glass of wine, even before I carried suitcases upstairs. *Tomorrow I will unpack my book bag full of summer reading and arrange them on my writing desk in the family room downstairs.*

Opening the living room's glass sliders and standing at the deck's railing, I drew in as much of the life-sustaining Cape air as my lungs would allow. *Breathe. Allow the utter silence to penetrate deep within you. It will make you strong.* Standing silently, looking over the overgrown abandoned cranberry bog toward the magnificent bay, I thought of how often that bay had spiritually sustained my soul through many of life's difficult passages. As I looked at the brilliant crimson sun slipping slowly into the leaden blue of the bay and listened to the sweet symphony of song birds retiring for the night, I made myself a promise to use this sacred isolation as an inward pilgrimage to find myself.

I poured a glass of wine, listening to the Indian flutes of my favorite Nakai CD, and rummaged through my canvas bag for a notebook. I quickly jotted down some of the issues which had popped into my head during the drive. Issues to be further explored: homesickness, self-confidence, conditional versus unconditional love, mother-daughter relationships, marital challenges, God issues, my "saving rabbits syndrome," loss and mourning.

I returned to the deck to await nature's inevitable ceiling of stars as they emerge from the night sky. Few places left on earth have an almost total absence of reflected light, allowing those observing their brilliance to feel as though they can reach up and pull them down to earth. The Cape sky is one of my most treasured possessions, for it never fails to lift my soul heavenward.

As the first and brightest star emerged from the darkness, I wondered if it could be the light from my sister's soul. I began to weep uncontrollably. Through my tears, I turned my face toward the stars and spoke out loud to her, "Truly, Joannie, you lived your life as if you were an angel while you were here on earth. Surely, if there is a heaven, that most brilliant of stars in this magnificent sky radiates in tribute to your journey here on earth." Only the distant ebb and flow of the sea penetrated the silence. I stood, with my eyes turned heavenward, allowing the sounds of the sea to enfold my bleeding heart. I lost all sense of time and place.

Suddenly, hearing the high-pitched whine of hungry mosquitoes, I dashed for the door. Realizing that I had not eaten all day, I scrounged around in the pantry and came up with some mixed nuts and smoked oysters. *How perfect. I'll carry my snacks upstairs with my wine, unpack the essentials, and drop into bed.* As I slowly climbed the stairs, I again thought how blessed I was to be able to ignore time, ignore responsibilities and simply resonate to my own rhythms.

Finishing my snacks and looking at the unpacked bags, I thought, *"Oh Lord, I don't have the strength left to unpack all this stuff. I'll just hang up the things that will wrinkle by morning, quite possibly pour myself a second glass of wine to take to bed with me and then pray that sleep will come."*

As I reached in one of the bags to hang up my summer sundresses, I saw the dreamcatcher, a special gift that my eight-year-old granddaughter Payton had given me just before I left home. Carefully I removed the bubble wrap, and with eyes brimming with tears, hugged it against my heart. "I love you Payton, I love you," I whispered into the silence. I hung it over the lampshade's finial, where it would be the last thing I saw at night and the first thing I saw in the morning.

I ran downstairs to turn off the lights, dashed upstairs, donned my favorite powder-blue-silk nightgown and snuggled into bed. Propped up on pillows, sipping my wine, I thought about Payton and studied her magical creation that dangled from the lamp beside my bed. Brown folded cardboard, about six inches in length and an inch wide, had been carefully wrapped with purple yarn to constrain the cardboard into pincer-like tongs. A long purple lanyard was designed to hang around the neck, or in this case, around my lamp's finial.

I could picture Payton in her downstairs craft room. An image emerged of Payton's silky blonde head bent in serious concentration with bright blue eyes flashing as she crafted a dreamcatcher to drive away evil spirits that frightened her during the night. She and I had spent many wonderful hours crafting together, she the teacher guiding and grading; me the student carefully following her instructions. I could hear her say, as she presented me with her gift, "Damma, Mommy told me you are having bad dreams because you miss your sister and are very sad. I made this dreamcatcher to throw away my bad dreams, but I want you to have it now. When you have bad dreams you can grab them, run to the window, and throw them away."

"Your gift is so wonderful, Payton. I will do exactly as you say, grab any bad thoughts, run to the window and throw them away. When I am frightened, Payton, I will think of you. But, what will you do, sweetheart, to drive away your nightmares?"

"I'll be OK, Damma. Herbert, my snake friend, sleeps in my bedroom now. I told Herbert that I was going to give you my dreamcatcher, and he has promised to protect me." Fighting back tears, I marveled at the magical thinking of childhood.

As I lay in my bed, I too engaged in a bit of magical thinking, wishing with all my heart that I could run to the open window with my dreamcatcher, grab my sister's soul from the night sky and pull her back to me. But I knew otherwise. I had read in a pamphlet from St. Joseph's Indian School in South Dakota that Native Americans of the Great Plains believe the air is filled with both good and bad dreams so they hang dreamcatchers in their dwellings and on their baby's cradle boards. According to legend, good dreams pass through the center hole to the sleeping person, but bad dreams are trapped in the web, where they perish in the light of dawn.

As my body moved towards sleep, I reached out and touched Payton's dreamcatcher hanging by my pillow in the moonlight. I wondered which demons I might find trapped in the web in the morning.

During the night, I awakened, feeling anxious and alone. I reached for Payton's dreamcatcher, and looking out the crescent-shaped bedroom window I could still see that brightest of stars. My beloved sister seemed to be telling me that after four years of mourning, it was time to let her go, time to re-embrace life fully, and move on. I knew with the coming of dawn, the star's light would diminish, but never disappear from the night sky or from my heart. It was indeed time to move from grief through mourning, to make peace with the loss of my sister. Blessed sleep returned.

"I was standing on . . . shifting ground . . . undertaking a new passage . . . confronting the lost and counterfeit places within {me} and releasing {my} deeper, innermost self–{my} true self. Change-winds called {me} to come home to {myself}, to become who {I} really {am}."

Sue Monk Kidd

CHAPTER TWO

A SISTER'S LIGHT

*D*awn came. The permissive solitude of my Cape house began loosening tense muscles, relaxing taut ligaments, and releasing a stoic facade. Embraced by the morning sunlight, I listened to the silence and felt my body begin to let go of the world's expectations of me.

Checking Payton's dreamcatcher for demons caught during the night but finding none, I dressed, anxiously wondering if closely examining my mother and sister's recent deaths would reopen other unexamined emotional and spiritual traumas from years past. Nevertheless, I felt my spirit begin its journey inward, slipping past accumulated scar tissue towards the black hole that I had never fully drained. Stored, festering accumulated pain; questions never asked, answers insufficient, fear and anxiety never confronted.

Determined to embrace whatever the day would bring, I pledged to confront more boldly my demons and dragons. I shuddered in anticipation of a quest that would lead me into darkness. I could only hope that it would ultimately lead me back into the light.

Downstairs, sunshine illuminated the living room, making paintings and furniture radiate as if in a seventeenth century Vermeer painting. As I rushed to the glass sliders, I witnessed a natural landscape glowing in vibrant colors: a foreground of vividly green cranberry bushes amidst deep green cedars, cream-colored sandy dunes intermittently sprinkled with gracefully waving emerald beach grasses. The dark shimmering bay and violet blue sky seemed to beckon me to come and walk awhile amidst the masterpiece.

Walking to the harbor for breakfast, smelling the wild grape vine's delicious aroma that never failed to make me salivate and think of my mother's homemade grape jam, I thought about the grape vine's clinging dependency that often threatens to squeeze the life out of the very supports so essential to its growth and well-being. Thoughts of my mother's gifts, often diminished by her clinging emotional dependency, surfaced. *Beware the Trojan horse that conceals enormous consequences,* I cautioned.

With the sun and soft ocean breezes in my face, and what seemed to be every conceivable variety of bird singing in celebration of this wondrous morning, I ambled down the back road, designated "Tommy's Road" in memory of my stepfather. The road leads past summer cottages, along an inlet filled with wild grasses and inhabited by a pair of gracefully nesting white swans. In the distance, the inlet provides a view of a classically-steepled white clapboarded church and the harbor. One of my family's favorite breakfast places, The Marshside, overlooks this postcard-perfect New England scene.

Walking home after a delicious breakfast of corn-beef-hash and eggs, my thoughts returned to my stepfather, Tommy. He rose early and walked this road for twenty summers before he died. He would say he was going for breakfast and coffee, but we all knew the real attraction was listening to the locals in their distinctive New England brogue talking of lobstering, fishing, boats, and tides. I suspect his daily walk provided Tommy with a respite from my mother's ever vigilant, and often times critical oversight, as well. Cape Cod gave this Irish coal miner's handsome son the freedom to just be. I always considered his visits as a spiritual exchange between his Irish soul and mine. I never walk "Tommy's Road" alone; he is always with me.

On the return from breakfast as I approached the Cape house, I began to tremble, anticipating the difficult task of directly confronting my sister's loss. But, I knew there was no alternative. *How do I do this? Where do I begin?* I hoped the large bag filled with books, which I had designated as my summer reading, might hold the answers.

Settling at my desk in the cottage's lower level, I began aligning books at random: loss and sacredness, faith and philosophy, what is painful and what is essential to living a full and informed life.

Next, I began to organize a plethora of papers I had written in 1989 at age forty-nine, while completing my undergraduate degree. Then I stacked papers that I had written twenty-nine years before while completing a junior college degree . . . before marriage . . . before children. An amused smile crossed my face as I remembered rereading both sets of papers, concluding that a certain amount of wisdom does indeed come with age.

Lastly, I began the arduous task of sorting through hundreds of miscellaneous bits and pieces of collected notations. I always have had a curious habit of documenting what I considered wise and insightful thoughts on any orphaned scrap of paper: napkins, torn corners of various program handouts, the backs of restaurant placemats and even a scrap of toilet paper! The many notations regarding books and articles read and treasured, along with personal insights garnered over the years lay before me.

Amidst the stack I came upon a raggedly torn scrap of paper which read, "I opened my eyes, and there was my angel." Instantly, memories I had so carefully tucked away sent shock waves against the walls of my conscious mind and transported me back in time.

I recalled driving home feeling exhausted, having spent a long day working at the Governor's residence in my capacity as Executive Director of The First Lady of Pennsylvania's Children's Partnership. I stopped at the hospital's dialysis unit, hoping to surprise my sister Joan and to share a tiny part of her devastating ordeal. Joan was an extremely proud and private person, so I knew that she would never ask me to come. She had always been stoic when under duress, unaccustomed to allowing others inside her heart, never at ease asking for help. I had hoped my visit would not be too invasive, but rather provide solace. I prayed that Joan would be able to lower her well-fortified drawbridge and let me into her heart.

I remembered thinking as I walked towards the hospital's entrance about our childhood home which had often spoken to me of unconditional love, but which quite frequently demonstrated otherwise. I thought about how children, totally dependent upon adults for well-being, try to reconcile unconditional rhetoric with a conditional environment and unconsciously begin to develop a fight, flight or freeze mentality. And, in doing so, turn inward, building protective complex emotional walls and spending time strategically planning effective escape routes. Stoicism, emotional self-sufficiency, often becomes protective cover.

Joannie's stoicism had morphed into an emotional fortress from which she could not escape. She could not ask for help, could not trust that those who claimed to love her truly did. Her gentle simplicity and loving spirit required an inordinate amount of protection from my mother's more aggressive and invasive spirit. Rather than do battle with Mother, my sister chose to withdraw behind well-fortified emotional walls.

Entering the dialysis unit, with my heart loudly thumping in my chest, I quietly approached Joan's chair. She opened her eyes, smiled, and said, "I open my eyes and there is my angel." I was so thankful I had decided to come. Until that moment, I never knew that my sister considered me her angel. My heart felt touched by Light.

Joan had been in the hospital many times, insisting that her husband not let me know when she had been admitted, "not wanting to burden me." As a result, I remained diligent about quietly tracking her whereabouts and simply showing up. It was as if we were caught up in some kind of emotional game of hide and seek. She would not ask; I would prove how much I loved her by never failing to track her down.

Joan spoke matter-of-factly of her battle with the disease saying that the discomfort caused by amputations and dialysis was minimal. But the loss of her eyesight and incontinence had greatly weakened her resolve to continue the fight. She expressed her agony at having lost control over her life. This is, however, with one exception—a personal choice to remove herself from dialysis would bring a relatively peaceful death in a week to ten days. A personal choice for her; a devastating blow to me. As she spoke, it felt as if pieces of my heart were plummeting into some dark and irretrievable crevasse.

Joannie remarked how often Mother had spoken about surviving the loss of her husband at an early age, and how she said she could never survive the loss of one of her children. In a very dark corner of my heart overwhelming and fearful questions began to grow. *Had Joan been planning all along to hold on only long enough to spare Mother the agony of seeing her worst fear materialize?* Joan knew that Mother, at eighty-seven, was a walking time bomb. Mother, having undergone open-heart surgery at seventy-three, had recently denied surgical intervention for a large abdominal aneurysm.

Could it be that I will lose my mother only to be closely followed by the death of my sister? What would happen to me if these two very significant women, who have always been a part of my life, simply disappear and I have no way of being with them? Will I be able to survive another seemingly bottomless pit of sorrow like I felt so many years ago when my father disappeared from my life? I determined that I would see both Mother and Joan several times a week to keep their spirits and hopes high. *If I laugh with them and love them enough, and ask God for healing often enough, surely they will be fine.*

I tamped down a throbbing, panicked loneliness that erupted in the darkest corner of my heart. *My mother was eighty-seven years old. OK. But, my beloved sister at sixty-three? No, absolutely not! But, I have screamed NO once before . . . when my father died at forty-seven.* At twelve years old, I had tried to bargain with God: I would devote the rest of my life to His service if He would let my father live. Those prayers went unanswered and caused my heart to wonder if God could hear me. *Now, with my sister's well-being in jeopardy, would God again remain silent? Does God exist? I agonized. Unassisted, how will I help Joan protect her vulnerabilities from further insults? Is the ultimate human challenge to accept that we are indeed on our own?*

Sitting at my Cape house desk with Joan now gone, I began to think about Joannie's dreams, how they had always been simple dreams of her wedding day, of babies, of a home of her own, of receiving Mother's acceptance and approval. She had asked so little of the world, only that it accept her unadorned and honest spirit. How many gifts she had given to others by accepting them just as they were. I thought about her quiet strength as she nursed my father and guided her three younger siblings while Mother scrambled to find a way to financially support her family. Joannie's wedding day dreams had been transformed from gossamer gown and glass slippers to navy blue shoes and a navy dress she had to purchase herself.

Joan had promised Mother that she would complete college before marriage so her decision to withdraw from college after her freshman year infuriated Mother. Joan persevered, got a job to pay for her meager wedding and struggled to accept Mother's adamant refusal to support her decision. Mother reluctantly attended Joan's wedding. Joan resented but ultimately reconciled the loss of her Cinderella dreams. She often stopped in front of churches waiting for the bride and her attendants to emerge "to see their beautiful gowns and floral bouquets." On my wedding day with Joannie as my Matron of Honor, I could sense her happiness for me and her sadness for her loss.

I thought about how happy Joan had been when her children were young and her home was a warm and nurturing refuge. Whenever I visited Joannie, even though she and I were very different, I always felt confirmed and at peace. I treasured her heart. We had often talked about how when we grew old together, we would tell silly stories and do silly things like riding into the sunset together in a big old white Cadillac convertible, with carefully selected soul sisters, listening to 50's tunes, and telling lots of lies. I had spent a lifetime assuming that she would always be part of my life. I began to realize that her sunset would precede mine. That I would have to face my own sunset without this wonderful source of solace and strength.

As all these memories ricocheted off the edges of my mind, I buried my head in my arms on the desk and wailed myself empty.

CHAPTER THREE

ENCOUNTERING
WISDOM AT THE
WATER'S EDGE

As the intensity of my grief slowly subsided, I realized I needed to walk towards a source of light. I donned my old sweater and headed down the sandy road to the beach, seeking solace in the timeless beauty and wonder which surrounded me. I knew that the water's hypnotic ebb and flow, the sheer beauty of sand and surf, the constancy represented by nature's magic, and her beach creatures would help ease my pain.

Humans seem drawn to the contemplative respite and wonder of the sea, as if we are in a constant lifelong struggle to recapture the overwhelming embryonic sense of total safety and peace we knew in the intrauterine sea within our mother's bodies, before conflict and pain, before doubt. As if the bay understood the need for that respite from my internal struggles, she tossed onto her beach one of her most ancient and fascinating creatures. There, sitting quietly but steadfastly in my path was a living fossil, an ancient survivor, a horseshoe crab. It was as if the bay were speaking to me of adaptation and survival in an often hostile world. I sat cross legged in the sand, questioning this remarkable creature about vulnerability, survival and tenacity.

Anyone who has taken the time to examine this strange armored creature knows that its underbelly is its only real vulnerability. When I turned her over on her back, exposing that vulnerability, she flailed her legs and long thin claws. She stiffened her spiny tail in a struggle to upright herself. Life has certainly turned me over on my back, I thought; so I, like my horseshoe crab friend, must fight as long as it takes to right myself.

I stared into her eyes embedded into the helmet-like shell, and whispered, "You have nothing to fear from me, little one. I know that many of you are being used for medical research, bled each year of your adult life for your blue, copper-based blood. I also know that ten to twenty percent of you die each summer as a result. So, amazing ancient creature, even though you have survived for more than two hundred million years, there is no guarantee that these new challenges will not ultimately destroy you. Stay vigilant, amazing survivor. Stay vigilant."

I tapped softly on her back, and as if she had heard me, within seconds, she had buried herself in the sand. I could not help but smile at how adept she had become in protecting her vulnerabilities from hostile outside forces. *I too need to develop greater awareness of my vulnerabilities and how best to protect myself from those forces that would do me harm. Hostile forces, both external threats as well as internal demons, can only do harm if allowed.*

As dusk settled over the beach, my fossil friend cautiously reemerged. As she scuttled back towards the sea, I called out to thank her for the reminder that every creature has vulnerabilities that may or may not be overcome. That every creature must accept its inconsequential link in a long ancestral progression. When this magical sea creature disappeared into the water's depths, I rose, brushed sand off of my shorts, and silently thanked her for lessening my anguish.

It takes great tenacity to right oneself when life unexpectedly turns upside down. Sometimes retreating into a safe and secure place until danger has passed is best. She knew when to struggle, when to retreat, and when to walk away. I suspect my crab friend has practiced this often; unfortunately, I have not. But, if I practice long enough, hopefully, I will learn to right myself with the same determination and grace. To know when to struggle, when to retreat, and when to walk away.

"The world breaks everyone
and afterward
many are stronger
at the broken places."

Ernest Hemingway

"Listening means hearing the voice
within you. It never fails to tell you the
truth, even if you don't want to hear it."

Nancy Wood | DANCING MOONS

CHAPTER FOUR

GRIEVING
LESSONS

U walked the long way home, down to Corporation Beach and back. As dusk turned to darkness, Joannie's star re-emerged.

In 1952, the year Dad died, Mother entered the workforce to support her four children, then ages eight through sixteen. Joan, the oldest, assumed many of the household responsibilities. She also struggled to come to grips with the reality that the champion who would do battle for Joan with a strong and determined mother, was gone. Dad's unconditional love and acceptance, something my mother was never able to give her, provided Joan with the space needed to discover her own uniqueness. But when Dad died she was left standing alone, a non-confrontational nature in a confrontational environment.

With her protector gone, Joan's sense of vulnerability led her to develop a very complicated and conflicted love relationship with Mother. Knowing how Mother believed that matriarchal power entitled her to define her children as she saw fit, Joan came to understand that the only way she could avoid confrontation and minimize vulnerabilities was to retreat deep within her private internal spaces. To the outside world, she appeared content and happy; however, like the horseshoe crab, she had developed an alert internal vigilance against unwelcome intruders. She knew when to struggle, knew when to retreat, and knew when to walk away.

Joan, with two sons ages eighteen and fifteen, discovered that she was pregnant again at thirty-eight. She was astounded but delighted. She determined that she and her new baby daughter would find a peaceful retreat from the pretentiousness of the world as she knew it. A place where you didn't need to pretend you were something other than who you were. Joan's husband presented her with the perfect gift . . . a cabin in the woods a stone's throw from the Girl Scout camp she loved and the lake that held sweet memories of family outings before Dad died. Joan retreated there almost every weekend, rain or shine, delighting in the freedom to be herself, anticipating that her two married sons would visit when they could, and immersing her daughter in her unpretentious world.

For many years Joan appeared to have finally made peace with who she was; meanwhile, Mother critically disapproved of both the cabin and her new-found friends, feeling the environment and her neighbors were not appropriate to Joan's station in life. Joan sensed Mother's disapproval, but as she had done so often in her life, chose to live her life without her approval. For a decade, Joan immersed herself in her magical retreat.

During a visit to the mountain cabin, Joan noticed a small blister on the toe of her right foot. Believing that she had merely stubbed her toe on a rock while swimming in the lake, she drove to the local Laundromat to attack the mounds of dirty bed linens left in the wake of weekend guests. By the time the first load was in the dryer, the blister's pain had substantially increased. She put her wet laundry in the car and drove to the nearest hospital emergency room.

The young intern looked at her foot and said, "We will probably be able to save your foot, but I'm not sure about the toe." Joan began to laugh hysterically, thinking, of course, that it was a joke. He told her he would admit her immediately to begin treating her diabetes. She assured him he would do no such thing; she would go home to consult with her own doctor and, if necessary, be admitted to the local hospital. He reiterated that she needed immediate attention and that he would call ahead to make the necessary arrangements.

Joan drove back to her cabin to pick up her husband, daughter and their two dogs. She waited until she was close to home before telling her husband that she needed to see the doctor. The doctor, upon examination, immediately admitted her to the hospital.

My mother, my younger sister Joyce, and I were scheduled to go to the shore for vacation. Joan, typically not wanting to inconvenience anyone, insisted that we follow through with our plans. "It's no big deal. Merely a blister on my toe," she said. Mother and Joyce went to the shore. I stayed with Joan. Joan railed against my decision, but I hung on, determined to support her through whatever lay ahead.

The doctors removed the toe's inflamed and dying skin, and Joan and I laughed about her mutant skinny toe. At first Joan was hesitant to allow me to look at it because she didn't want to upset me and besides, she said, "It wasn't really any big deal. It really doesn't even hurt." To penetrate her stoicism and express my empathy, I told her that I wanted to see her toe . . . that it was important that I see . . . that I feel. How else would I be able to effectively support her? She relented. Raising the sheet from her foot I glanced at her face to make sure I was not adding to her angst. Her facial expressions confirmed what she could not orally express: relief and gratefulness.

As Joannie slept, I thought about life's lessons learned; *fully participating in another's pain and suffering builds strong internal spaces that serve one well in times of great distress, a kind of emotional reservoir from which one can drink whenever necessary. Suffering fills emotional reservoirs with empathy, courage and strength.* At this point in my life, I was growing in my conviction that cumulative suffering does not snuff out internal Light, it increases the Light's intensity, while teaching us how best to draw on its strength in order to share it with others, making this a much less lonely world.

As I watched my sister sleep, I thought about human vulnerabilities and strengths. *Life is temporary. Humans are extremely fragile, both physically and emotionally. Maybe there is nothing external to our beings that can quiet our anxiety and keep us safe. Maybe life's challenge is all about growing strong, safe places within ourselves as a shelter from pain and suffering. Maybe each of us is our only keeper. Maybe each of us is in charge of what we allow the world to do to us.*

When Joan awakened, we talked briefly about how pain-free she felt. Both she and I naively took solace in her lack of pain following the surgery. Joannie told me that her doctor had explained that most likely she had been diabetic for about ten years before the blister appeared. "I do not have diabetes," she declared. "The doctor is wrong."

Trying to make sense out of her denial, I wondered if she believed that in acknowledgment she would somehow empower the disease. Or, did Joan believe that the strength of her formidable will, which had defeated most adversaries, would ultimately destroy this demon as well? I began to suspect that Joan had not had a thorough physical exam in ten years. *Had she been ignoring subtle signs for years? Had she no way of knowing that the killer was silently destroying her body before it announced its presence by erupting from her toe?*

Uncomfortable with any further discussions about her health, Joan shifted the conversation. We spoke about some local issues and I took my leave, telling her that I would return tomorrow.

Arriving home from the hospital, I immediately marched to my computer to google diabetes research. If I knew how to slow its progress and shared that understanding with Joan, maybe she would be able to better understand her disease and be more willing to take the necessary steps to defeat it. My research disclosed that the lack of pain was an indication that her disease had progressed to the point where it was damaging her nerve endings and thus her ability to feel. Numbness is one of the only consolations this heinous disease offers to its victim; it slowly, but steadily, kills off a body's ability to heal itself. Most likely the disease had already extensively damaged her body. Sheer terror began to grow in a corner of my mind.

I knew I would not share this discouraging knowledge with Joan, but would do everything I could to encourage her to take the recommended steps necessary to slow down the disease's progression. I would never know if Joan's doctors had fully explained her circumstances, as she never shared any doctor's office conversations.

Once her toe began to heal, she was given a large blue protective boot to wear home. We laughed often and at great length about her starting a whole new fashion trend, all the while not talking about our greatest fears. Having read everything I could get my hands on regarding diabetes, I tried to encourage her to exercise, to be diligent about her diet, and to test her glucose levels.

She continued to deny she had the disease and used one of Mother's dictums to express how she felt, "The damn doctors don't know what they are talking about." She continued to live her life as she had always done—eating what she wanted, doing a minimum of exercise, and continuing to smoke. Having read that smoking substantially increases the risk of amputation for diabetics, I told Joan I simply could not watch her smoke. She stopped smoking in front of me, but each time we got together the smell of smoke served to remind me of her refusal to do what was necessary to save herself. I continued to agonize about how I might persuade her to take control of her disease. To no avail.

Arriving back at the Cape house, I stepped into the outdoor shower to wash the sand from my feet and all I could see in my mind's eye were Joannie's slender, gracefully arched bare feet. I pushed the image of her stripped mutant toe from my mind. "No," I said aloud, "tonight I want to celebrate my lovely sister by remembering her whole." How much she loved being barefoot from early spring through summer and how Mother had always said she had the most beautiful feet in the family. I pictured her in a swimsuit coming out of the lake with a deep golden tan, and a breathtaking smile, exposing perfectly aligned flashing white teeth. Her black eyes danced with laughter and her jet black hair sparkled with sunlight. I could hear my father's voice calling to her, "Black Beauty, put on some shoes or you will cut your feet again. Remember when you jumped across the stream and landed on a broken bottle? Come on now, put on some shoes."

Standing on the deck with my arms raised to the sky, I tearfully whispered into the night, "Joannie, sweet sister, I miss you so. Why are you not here washing the sand from between your toes? Why are we not able to spend the evening reading and talking about books we love and sharing stories about our precious grandchildren? Why? I just don't understand. How could you simply have disappeared from my life? Where in the hell are you? Amidst my love for you, I feel anger, Joan, anger that you refused to take charge of your disease when there was still time to do so. Loss, sorrow and anger pound at my heart. It's so complicated to feel anger amidst sorrow towards you, but my heart is ravaged with the love/anger dilemma. Why couldn't I save you? Why wouldn't you save yourself?"

Exhausted and not feeling like I could eat, I climbed the stairs with a glass of wine, sat it on the edge of the shower and prayed that the cool water would bring some peace to my tortured soul. "For an agonizing four years you have been gone, and I still struggle to rearrange my heart to accommodate your absence," I said into the water. In the deepest recesses of my heart, I wondered anew if I had done enough to save her. *What if I had stopped work earlier, so I could have spent more time with her? What if I had more aggressively argued with her about her decision to ignore her plight? What had so damaged her heart that she had been unwilling to acknowledge her disease and make the sacrifices necessary to save herself? What if I had read to her so she could have better understood the nature of the killer that lived inside of her?*

Could I have saved her forever lodged into my soul.

I climbed into bed listening to the melodic sound of the bog peepers celebrating the night, and told myself, "Damn it, Janet, she is gone. Give it up. You did what you could do. Most importantly, when she lay dying she knew how much you loved her. She carried that love with her on angel's wings. Let it go."

As I fell asleep, I remembered my therapist's words: "Allow yourself to mourn; it is so essential to well-being. Don't let those around you dictate a timeframe. Losing a mother disorients us. To have lost a mother, and then seven months later, your sister is devastating. You have every right to feel as you do, rudderless and vulnerable. Take the time to mourn the loss of your world as you knew it."

CHAPTER FIVE

A GIFT
TWICE GIVEN

From past experiences, I instinctively knew that the next steps in the mourning process would be the most difficult to bear—fully accepting the death of a loved one and moving on with life. I was not yet prepared to fully engage that next step. As I had done so often in my life, I turned to books; their transformative power and thoughtful insights always provide meaningful glimpses into my internal landscapes. Desperately needing wise counsel to support my journey, I hoped that the books I had brought with me would indeed assist in quieting and then nurturing my soul. I ran downstairs to my desk and randomly selected one of the books I had brought along to read, Gail Sheehy's *Passages*.

As I sat wrapped in the warmth of a golden summer sun pouring through the windows of the sunroom, I settled more deeply into my favorite red leather recliner. Listening to spiritual-soft Nakai music and smelling the rich aroma of a mug of freshly-brewed coffee perched on the arm of my chair, I opened the cover of *Passages*. Suddenly, my eyes locked onto Joannie's signature and the date July 1976. My head fell back against the chair's pillow as my eyes closed and I gasped for air. *Your distinct signature, so uniquely you, Joan, makes me feel as if you are here with me. I want so deeply to keep my eyes closed, to believe you are still beside me.* Slowly re-opening my eyes, the same devastating feeling of profound loss returned to my heart.

I thought about the significance of the 1976 date. Twenty-eight years ago Joan had given me this book, long before diabetes began to steal her life, and I felt an overwhelming need to turn back time so she and I could redirect events to save her. Through my tears, my index finger began to trace her signature, letter by letter, as if in doing so, it would somehow tangibly reconnect me to her, help me to touch her one more time. Kissing the tip of my index finger and retracing her signature again, I wondered which parts of the book had spoken most powerfully to her, which ideas helped to heal her wounded spaces, which concepts challenged or confirmed her long-held beliefs.

Slowly, I began to realize that, like her star, the signature reached out to me, trying to tell me something. I pressed the book containing microscopic pieces of her DNA to my chest and whimpered, "No, I don't want to let you go. You have to stay with me. I want so desperately to see you, talk with you," I said aloud through my tears. "Where are you, Joannie? Are you somewhere? Is there a somewhere? Are you OK? Do you know how much I love you even after death?"

I waited in silence. Suddenly, text from a song written by the St. Louis Jesuits surged into my mind, "All I ask of you is forever to remember me as loving you." I felt a surge of gratitude that we had spent time together before she died, time to express to each other how deeply we loved one another. Emerging from somewhere deep inside was the understanding that the beauty of our gifts to one another would have to sustain me, for she indeed was gone.

As a deep sense of loneliness threatened to overwhelm me, I grabbed my journal from the table beside me and began to write. Much time elapsed as I wrote a sort of good-bye letter to my sister. Once I finished my journal entry, I felt a sense of completion. It was as if, after holding my breath in a survival mode for so long, I had finally managed to break through the roiling seas of mourning and resurfaced into the life renewing ocean air. I could feel my sister's permissive arms releasing me. *"Live, Janet, live for both of us,"* I heard her whisper.

When I finished writing, I sat immobilized.

Slowly I began to realize I was starved! Rooting around in the freezer, I managed to uncover some bread which I quickly defrosted in the microwave, and a can of tuna from the pantry. I made myself a sandwich and poured myself a coke. I smiled— one of Joan's favorite lunch combinations. If only I had a bag of potato chips, it would be perfect. As I discovered an unopened bag of chips in the back of the cupboard, I felt a celebratory surge remembering all the tuna fish sandwich lunches Joan and I had shared together. *You will always have sweet memories of Joan that you can pull, at will, into your heart whenever you need her near you.* I felt a glimmer of peace begin to stir deep inside my heart.

After lunch, my thoughts returned to *Passages.*

"A book burrows into your life
in a very profound way
because the experience
of reading is not passive."

Erica Jong

"The way we talk to our children
becomes their inner voice."

Peggy O'Mara

CHAPTER SIX

JOUSTING WITH DEMONS
AND DRAGONS

I had read *Passages* twenty-eight years ago.

I settled myself into the red leather recliner, placed my journal on the wide wooden arm of the chair, intending to jot down those issues which felt most relevant to my current struggle. *Which issues feel strikingly alien and in need of further exploration? Which issues trigger nervous curiosity? Which insights signal my internalized demons to prepare for battle?* I knew from my previous reading that Sheehy was about to provide the battle plan, and it would be up to me to suit up and go forth to slay my dragons. I wrote at the top of my journal page, "Insights and Strategies for Destroying Demons and Dragons."

I began to read *Passages* in earnest. In the first chapter, Sheehy writes about the difficult "work" of adult life, about the healing art of self-examination, the universally-experienced developmental rhythms and predictable crises, as well as the crucial shifts that must occur for growth.

I welcomed the idea that self-examination ultimately leads to healing and that if I persevered, healing would eventually occur. I desperately needed that reassurance. I wrote predictable and crucial in my journal, adding if crises are predictable and shifts crucial to growth, then I must conclude that all humans share similar predictable developmental passages, similar suffering. *Everyone suffers; it is an integral part of life. Maybe the ultimate question is, "What do you do with suffering?"*

As I reread what I had written, I felt the intensity of my own losses—deaths of my father, mother, sister and nephew, loss of first love, loss of youth. The intensity of personal struggles—navigating marital difficulties, lovingly rearing children, and having to give up long-held dreams. As I wrote the list in my journal, I realized again that my experiences, my suffering, were not unique but just another iteration of humankind's challenging cyclical journey. By holding my own experiences up to the light of universal suffering, I felt their intensity diminish.

I turned my attention back to *Passages*.

"With each passage some magic must be given up, some cherished illusion of safety and comfortably familiar sense of self must be cast off to allow for the greater expansion of our distinctiveness."

Magic? I was uncertain what myths, what "magic" I needed to give up to grow myself, but the idea of having to give up magical thinking intrigued me. *Have I held onto the "magic" of childhood, distorting memories and stunting my ability to fully participate in adult relationships, to see life realistically? Have I, or someone else, created the myths, and why?* I vowed to pay particularly close attention to any magical delusions I uncovered as I moved more deeply into internal spaces. The notion of giving up magical thinking frightened me, for it meant shaking loose long-held delusions from my soul. But Sheehy said it's necessary if we are to see more clearly.

I added, "the necessity to give up magical thinking" to my journal's notations.

When I glanced out the window, I realized the gloriously sunny afternoon was quickly slipping away. I closed my book and journal, slipped a few dollars in my jeans pocket, donned my tortoise-shelled sunglasses and sneakers, and headed down our sandy road towards Route 6A.

As I made the sharp turn onto Tommy's Road and approached the sheep farm, I smiled thinking about the older couple, whose daughter, grandchildren and son-in-law lived across the road from them. A path cut into the meadow's high grasses allows grandchildren easy access to their grandparents' house and allows the grandparents' sheepherding Border collie access to their daughter's pastured sheep. In my many walks past the farm, I would see a flash of black and white fur dashing across the road, down the meadow path to check on whether his sheepherding skills are needed. A few moments later, having confirmed that his charges are well and his herding instincts not needed, the collie dashes back along the meadow path, collapsing by the farmhouse door.

Most days the grandparents can be seen working in the field behind their farmhouse, cutting flowers and harvesting acres of vegetables for sale at a small umbrella table along the road. A small handwritten sign invites a passersby to select from the table, leave money in a coffee can, and bag their purchases using a plastic recycled grocery store bag found in a flowered cotton bag holder suspended from the branch of a small fruit tree nearby. Each summer my heart remains suspended until I know the grandparents are in their garden, signaling that all is as it should be.

Is it as it should be or are my superficial observations just another instance of magical thinking?

As I stood contemplating life lived on this simple sheep farm, I was transported back in time to my family's farm, Barleycroft. My mind's eye saw thoroughbred horses jumping hurdles in a riding ring behind the barn, Black Angus steers and sheep grazing in the meadow, a large and bountiful vegetable garden, a beloved collie guarding all things important. I smelled manure, sweet meadow grasses, grapes dangling from an arbor, and the wonderful leather smell of saddles and bridles stored in the tack room. I heard loud peels of laughter ringing through the air as grandchildren raced each other to the lake. My family's farm differed from this small New England sheep farm, but when I came to buy flowers, I always saw the similarities of rhythm, vitality, family and celebration of life.

Those memories generated great joy in my heart.

Suddenly, thoughts of other times at Barleycroft erupted into my mind, times when conflict and anger, sadness and hostility permeated the air. My thoughts flew back to an early morning incident between my mother and grandfather. Home from college over spring break, I came down the steps for breakfast and overheard my mother say, "I have done everything I could to please you, take care of you, be a considerate daughter, and make you proud. All you can do is criticize me. I will not allow you to dictate to me how I should live my life. I don't care if you do not approve of drinking and parties. I don't care if you don't approve of staying up late and not rising at dawn. That is what I choose to do. No one has dictated to you how to live your life. You have made some wise decisions and some very unwise decisions. Stop trying to dictate to me how to live my life."

When I entered the kitchen, I saw my grandfather sitting in his usual seat at the end of the kitchen table looking out the window towards the barn, angrily tapping his fingers. Thinning grayish-blonde hair, stern Germanic blue eyes behind partially shell-rimmed glasses, frame a weathered face with a rigidly set jaw. Khaki shirt, khaki pants with a colorful tie make up his daily uniform. Suddenly, he turned to my mother with a terrifyingly aggressive look on his face. "You truly are your mother's daughter. Your mother insisted she knew best, too, and look where that got her. I resent that you invite her to visit the farm."

My mother, the mighty warrior, squared her broad shoulders and straightened her back to her full five-five height, and with furrowed brow and squinted eyes, shouted her call to battle. "You will not dictate to me how to live my life, who to invite into my home, the hour I should go to bed and when to get up in the morning. She is my mother and I will invite her here whenever I please. If you would rather not be here when she comes for a visit drive into town until she is gone. Your anger eats away at your soul and distorts everything you say and do. Move on for God's sake; her offenses happened a thousand years ago. Let it go."

I ran to within feet of my grandfather and shouted, "The best thing that ever happened in your life was to have my mother as your daughter. My mother is nothing like her mother. She is loving, loyal and responsible. You talk as if Mother did not suffer immeasurably all of her life because her mother deserted her. The one person in your life who has nurtured and protected you, saved your assets when the courts threatened to take every penny, cooked and cleaned for you, nursed you when you were ill, created Barleycroft and invited you to live with us. Barleycroft, the only real joy you have ever had in your life. Stop saying hateful things to my mother."

"Is that how you dealt with my beautiful, fun-loving Grandmother? No wonder she ran away. Was your obsessive rage against my grandmother the reason you shot Mother's pet dog when she was twelve and had nothing else to love, you simply had to take a pound of flesh from someone? Here we are again, this morning, with you reactively spewing forth your venom in some distorted effort to punish your daughter for the sins of her parents. How can you continue to blame your child for the hell you yourself created?" Accustomed to backing up my mother as she charged into battle against her often venomously aggressive father, I was not startled when those words came out of my mouth.

I was startled now by the eruption of painful Barleycroft memories, for I had so masterfully concealed them from my heart. Sheehy was right, I thought. If I am to grow myself and my most precious relationships, I must indeed give up some measure of magical thinking. I realized that for years I had been selectively creating a perfect Barleycroft, inhabited by a lovingly perfect birth family, and then had used that mythological perfection to measure all my future relationships. I felt gratitude towards Sheehy for helping me to see that neither people nor memories have to be perfect to be cherished. *Maybe accepting imperfections in myself and those I loved might free me to love myself and others more effectively. I must remain vigilant about identifying other magical thinking techniques that had limited my ability to see and to fully understand.*

As I gathered an armful of yellow and purple gladiolas and tucked dollars in the coffee can, I began to calculate how many summers I had repeated this blessed flower ritual. Thirty summers, I concluded. I felt so tickled that this wonderful couple allowed me to buy their beautiful bounty for a mere five dollars. Oh, seven dollars if you wanted a vase. Being able to buy such a labor-intensive product for a few dollars on an honor system told me a lot about the quality of their souls, shaped during simpler times, when civility, generosity, honor and integrity seemed to be more the rule and less the exception. A time that grew feelings of safety and connectedness with others. Of trust. Of compassion. *Could these visions of times past just be another instance of magical thinking?*

Then I asked myself, *"When exactly was the world a simpler and more humane place, Janet?"* From my childhood perspective, with its limited understanding and exposure to the broader world, life did indeed appear to be more humane and loving. But maturity, accompanied by a growing understanding of man's universal inhumanity to man, forced me to confront the historical slaughter of millions of innocents in the name of one God or another . . . one race, ethnicity, or clan.

"I suppose the notion of 'the good old days' is indeed just another iteration of magical thinking," I whispered.

As I turned for home, I wondered if Sheehy had been right about giving up magical thinking. *I think the challenge is to identify destructive magical thinking that inhibits your ability to grow, while retaining a modicum of magical thinking deep within your heart as a source of inspiration, possibility and hope.* Some magical thinking had indeed fueled my spirit; some had also inhibited my ability to see clearly. I needed to find the proper balance. In my heart, I felt certain that I could not confront my demons without some sense of spiritual magic and possibility.

As I thought further about spiritual magic, I realized that I had not consciously initiated this journey in search of self; the journey had become necessary because of seismic shifts deep inside me. Transformative shifts in my life were providing opportunities to explore who I am, and what is more important, who I might become. Rather than squander life's energies in pursuit of superficial external gains, those painful shifts seemed to be driving me inward, encouraging me to dedicate myself to growing a learned spirit of mindfulness, introspection and courage. I noted in my journal that grappling with the inside-outside duality of our lives is a long and arduous journey, but a journey which holds the promise of living an authentic life connected to one's spiritual core. Neither people nor memories have to be perfect. Find balance between destructive and constructive magical thinking.

Then I recalled a quote from Nancy Wood's *Dancing Moon* that I recently added to my journal. "Introspection is the key to understanding the conflict raging within you. Dig out the old fear and throw it away. Fill up your soul with pieces of beauty. Take time to knit them together. They will make you whole."

I went into the sunroom, turned off the lights and opened all the windows. Listening to the night sounds and watching stars appear in the lowering darkness, I thought about all the loved ones I had left behind at home and promised myself to call them to make sure everyone was fine. *I wonder if I will feel overwhelmed with homesickness if I hear their voices. I don't think so, not overwhelmed . . . not this time. Everyone seems to be so overjoyed with my adventure that they have given me the spiritual permission to just be. No guilt, just be. What an elegantly lovely gift from those you love.*

I arose to call home listening to the melody of late June bugs and moths skittering across the screens. Phil's voice resonated with warmth and loving care, and I knew all was well at home. We spoke for some time, catching up on family and friends, and how he and I were doing. I told him I needed to hear the girls' voices so I would be calling them also, and would email everyone from time to time to keep them apprised of my summer's wanderings. Phil told me how proud he was of my courage. I told him how grateful I was for his support. We hung up after a promise to talk again soon.

As I climbed the stairs, relieved that all was well at home, I made a mental note to go to the grocery store tomorrow since the pantry was becoming depleted. *Or, I could just alternate walking to Sesuit Harbor or Marshside Restaurant or The Lost Dog Pub for breakfast and dinner and skip lunch. It feels so liberating to have the freedom to choose when to eat, what to eat, or not to eat at all. I think I've come up with the perfect solution; I will cook occasionally, but eat out most of the time.*

Singing "I once was lost but now I'm found, was blind but now I see" at the top of my lungs, I showered and toweled off, pulled on a nightgown, squeezed Payton's dreamcatcher and fell asleep.

CHAPTER SEVEN

TAKING UP
THE SWORD

Next morning, I opened the bedroom windows, already feeling the heat of the day and popped my favorite yoga DVD into the video recorder. After groaning, stretching and breathing myself towards the very illusive goddess-like image I carried in my head, I trotted into the bathroom to take a shower. Catching a glimpse of myself in the wall of mirrors over the bathroom's double sink quickly destroyed any remnants of goddess illusions. *Hmm, just another piece of magical thinking,* I laughed to myself into the invigoratingly cool water. *Even if I want to hold onto goddess illusions, the wall of mirrors does not lie.*

Quickly dressing in shorts and a light summer shirt and donning my sunglasses, I half walked, half ran to breakfast at Sesuit Harbor Cafe, grabbed a quick egg and bacon on a bagel with an iced coffee, and hurried home. I was eager to return to reading *Passages.*

Extending the deck's electrified awning to shade me from the sun's intensity, I settled into the comfy lounge chair with a glass of lemonade, my journal and Sheehy's book. Sheehy wrote of the universal stages of crisis, loss, mourning, spiritual searching, and recovery. I noted the stages of mourning in my journal and then paused to question my place on Sheehy's continuum. I was locked in mourning.

I had mourned much in my life, but no one, until now, had helped me to understand the stages of grief. In my family the terrifying sense of loss felt each time a loved one died was stuffed somewhere deep inside, left to accumulate, to fester. And then, time moved on. *Our family's stoic motto might be "rabbits don't wail." Well, maybe rabbits should wail to make themselves whole again.* I felt pieces of emotional armor shift and loosen, in anticipation of an even deeper and more intense internal probe.

Sheehy wrote about the sanctuary of family, of leaving home emotionally and of the commands of others that have been partially incorporated into the self. But, feeling confused, I thought, Mother always told me to remember where I had come from, that loyalty to her and my sisters and brother was paramount. I have always struggled with homesickness whenever I have to be away from family. I felt Sheehy was telling me that to find myself, to overcome my debilitating homesickness, I must first liberate myself from the commands of my internalized "parent-custodian." I felt emotionally anxious about confronting my internalized Mother, but I knew in my heart I needed to do so.

Suddenly, a conversation with Joannie many years ago flashed into my mind. "You really tried to set yourself free during adolescence, Janet, but you failed. Mother's assertive power simply wore you down. I was always worried that once you gave in to her, you would never be free. Never find out who you really are." Like Sheehy, Joan was telling me that it was essential to liberate myself from Mother's dominance.

I knew in my heart they were right; my fear of Mother's disapproval was so strong that I came to believe that my mother's voice was mine, that she was more capable of making the right decisions for me. There was even a part of me that believed that I could not survive without her. I heard the distant rattle of the warrior donning her armor.

The phone ringing jolted me from the intensity of emotions I was feeling. Joyce Halpert, a dear friend and neighbor at the end of our road, extended a dinner invitation. "You have been holed up too long by yourself; join us for dinner and some good wine," she said. Being hesitant to break my momentum but knowing that time spent with the Halperts not only nurtured one's body, but also one's soul, I asked if we could dine together in a few days. Being a caring and sensitive friend, she told me to call them whenever I felt ready to take a break.

I decided the deck was too warm, even with the awning's shade. I grabbed my book and journal and moved inside. With *Passages* on my lap, I settled myself on the living-room couch which faces French doors and an expansive view of the bay. I found myself studying a large Harry Holl oil painting that hangs prominently on the living room's peaked wall. When I first saw the painting in Harry's studio, I knew I had to own it. The picture depicts an angular male face subtly emerging out of myriad shades of abstract blue surrounds, exhaling a soft orange breath. I call him Blue Spirit and hear him speaking to me about tenacity, courage, and adaptability in the face of life's adversities. Harry Holl had been a gifted potter all his life, but when challenged with Parkinson's and unable to continue potting, he shifted his talents from potting to oil painting at eighty years of age. When I look at this painting, I am not only reminded of Harry's tenacious courage and adaptability, but my mother's as well. She, too, had courageously adapted to life's many difficult demands and had demonstrated a resiliency of character and courage. The painting encourages me to live a colorful and bold life, to strive to live courageously.

Scargo Pottery, Harry's home, studio and retail shop is a short distance from my Cape house, so I walk there often. A large open-sided structure surrounded by outdoor kiosks displays handmade colorful ceramics of every description. Multicolored dinnerware, wall hangings, sculptural busts, castle-like birdhouses, bird feeders and birdbaths, wind chimes, and utilitarian pottery pieces of every description are displayed in a setting of beautiful flowers, a koi pond, and tall pines. Entering the main indoor gallery, senses continue to dance with enchantment—flowers floating in multi-colored vases, classical music softly playing, and colorful pottery interspersed with large, bold oil paintings. Two potters' wheels with working artists willing to talk with you about their creations add to the gentle, nurturing space. And of course, Harry, bent and shuffling but not deterred from embracing life fully, can usually be found creating his own art and mentoring younger artists.

Sometime soon I will wander down to see what's going on at Scargo Pottery, make sure Harry is OK, I thought. *Or, maybe I should wander down now, spend the rest of the afternoon watching the potters work, see if Harry's around, and then walk on to The Lost Dog for an early dinner? Procrastination in confronting my internalized Mother or just a good idea? Maybe a little bit of both . . . confronting Mother will come soon enough.*

I didn't see Harry when I arrived at Scargo, so, I inquired about his well-being. I felt assured when one of his daughters told me that he was off organizing a show at the local art museum. I sat on a wooden bench near the potters' wheels and watched the sometimes powerful, sometimes gentle manipulative pressure of the potters' hands center, throw and shape humps of clay into beautiful vases.

If Sheehy is right, my mother's internalized hands mold, shape, and manipulate my being every day. Maybe that's OK, as long as I balance her voice with my own. I am learning how to leave home by emotionally centering and shaping my being to better reflect my own vision and voice, so maybe there is no reason to continue to fear my internalized parent. Maybe her voice has been muted and balanced by my own and is no longer dangerous to my well-being. I will continue reshaping myself until a multicolored piece of art emerges from my hump of clay. I will have to be diligent about monitoring the power of Mother's internalized voice. Her voice often is constructive, while other times it feels frighteningly confrontational and destructive. I must explore all the facets of my mother's persona, unafraid and unintimidated, reminding myself that people you love don't have to be perfect.

As the potters' finished work, covering their clay creations with damp cloths to preserve elasticity for another day, I said my good-byes. I walked to The Lost Dog thinking about the necessity of preserving elasticity if I were to continue to mold and shape my being. I sat at one of the bar tables, had a glass of wine and a burger, and felt grateful that I was beginning to feel strong enough to confront my internalized mother-energy and seek to balance the intensity of her residual energy with my own. The tautness that throbbed across my shoulders and rippled downwards into the small of my back foretold the emotional challenges which lay ahead.

Walking home down Tommy's Road, just as the sun was withdrawing from the sky, thoughts of Joannie filled my mind. I promised myself I would call my daughters to touch base when I got home. I will be most eager to see them when the summer is over. I miss them terribly.

Susan was not home when I called, but I left a message telling her how much I loved her and that I was doing well. I asked her to call when she had a chance. Tracy and I chatted about granddaughters Victoria and Payton's swimming lessons, Victoria's enthusiastic participation in horseback riding lessons, and Tracy and Carl's fall plans to take the girls to Disney World. I spoke briefly with Payton and Victoria, telling them I missed and loved them very much. Before hanging up, I also told Tracy how much I loved her. "Love you too," she replied.

As I hung up, I thought about Tracy's very quiet and gentle personality, a personality rooted in enormous strength. Often, sensing that I have become ensnared by my need to save rabbits and thus unable to make painful choices, she reminds me to "Be strong, Mother." She has taught me a lot about tenacity and strength.

Years ago someone had suggested that I had not loved Tracy enough, that I had been too distracted and involved with my daughter Susan's struggles to adequately love Tracy. It made me sad to think that unintentionally I might have somehow let Tracy down. Mother often stressed how important it is to love all your children equally, even though she had not succeeded in doing so. Nevertheless, I felt guilty that I might have somehow failed Tracy. Painstakingly I came to understand that Tracy, even from a young age, had clearly defined private boundaries. An image of Tracy when she was a toddler standing with her arm raised at a ninety-degree angle with elbow extended to discourage anyone who wished to hug her popped into my mind. Even as a small child, those physical boundaries played a defining role in how she wished to be parented. As an adult, she continues to maintain physical and emotional boundaries, only allowing carefully selected loved ones access to her heart.

In time, I came to realize that, as parents, we love different personalities differently; and most significantly, if we are to parent successfully, we must allow the child to define their own emotional needs and how they wish to be loved. It is largely the child, not the parent, who defines the parameters of the parent-child relationship, a notion that my mother never understood. Mother insisted that she define the parameters of the parent-child relationship, never acknowledging the diverse emotional needs of her four children. As her children entered adulthood, Mother was never able to adjust the balance of power in the parent-child relationship. Parents tend to hold on to certitudes, unable to conquer the most difficult parental obligation . . . ceding power to their adult children.

A Jungian concept immediately popped into my mind . . .

"We cannot live the afternoon of life according to
the program of life's morning; for what was great in the
morning will be little at evening, and what in the morning was true will by evening have become a lie. Write
a new program for the afternoon of life."

*I am striving to write a new program. I wish with all my
heart that my mother had been able to do so. I no longer need a
parent in charge, I need a compassionate friend who is willing to
listen.* Mother listened with compassion but always as a parent in charge. As a consequence, her children struggled with
self-confidence and independence. Mother's childhood abandonment and complicated adolescence, combined with young
widowhood, created a driving need for control; she believed
being in charge ensured safety for herself and her children.

Going directly upstairs, I slipped into my nightgown,
brushed my teeth and washed my face, then propped myself up
on bed pillows to watch the final burst of the sun's rays as it
slipped silently into the bay. A deep sense of satisfaction emerged
as I realized I had managed to control quiet quivers of homesickness as I spoke to Tracy and my granddaughters. *Maybe homesickness is no longer such an overwhelmingly disabling malady. Amazing
progress being made, I thought, but a long walk still remains.*

I decided it was time to think further about the power
of internalized parents. I returned to *Passages.* Sheehy argues
that fear comes from the fear of "defying our inner custodian."
I had always feared success and failure but never understood

why. I certainly had been taught that my proper role was to please. Could fear of my internalized Mother be the reason that each time I struggle to assert my independence, my sense of risk feels overwhelming and an excruciating sense of guilt stops me in my tracks? Did I really fear my mother? That notion seemed preposterous. I loved her. Nevertheless, I added fear of inner custodian's disapproval to my journal.

I was startled by the notion that I should not feel guilty and disloyal as I challenge long-held beliefs about my mother, that confrontation with my inner custodian is essential if I am to reclaim myself. As the rabbit, I need to suppress my feelings of vulnerability and fear and allow the warrior's assertiveness to confront and disarm long-held truisms driven deep into my being by my warrior mother. I could not stop myself from thinking that if there is an afterlife, a heaven, then Mother must be furious with me. I felt a nauseating fear erupt in the pit of my stomach. *I love my mother and I do not want her to be furious with me, I whined inside myself.*

I have always thought of myself as a rabbit. *Do I really have a sufficiently assertive warrior side that will sustain me once the battle begins? Was Sheehy correct that my internal rabbit-warrior duality had caused divisions within myself, I wondered? If I am to heal my internal conflicts, confront my internalized demons, I must recognize my warrior and allow her to suit up for battle.* I felt like crying. I felt like giving up this internal search for me. What did it matter any way? I'm fine. I don't need to do this.

I put aside *Passages* and turned off the light, feeling uneasy and too exhausted to read further. Sensing a dangerous space enveloping me, I hoped sleep would come easily.

"Who was this self
inside of me
who cried out to be?"

Sue Monk Kidd

"Yesterday, today, and tomorrow
all live in the same room."

Bob Dylan

FILM *I'M NOT THERE*

CHAPTER EIGHT

SHARDS OF GLASS

A few hours later I lay wide awake, wondering what had awakened me. Listening for unusual house sounds and hearing none, I struggled to go back to sleep, but *Passages* excerpts about "guardian-dictators" and the controlling presence of "phantom parents," kept pounding away inside my mind. My mother, my "guardian-dictator," had died, yet her penetration of my being had been so complete I continued to struggle to free myself from her influence. I turned on the light, squeezed the dreamcatcher, got out of bed, grabbed my journal and a pen and sitting in the chair by the bedroom windows that face the bay, I began to write about my mother in light of insights I had garnered from my reading.

My mother had died in 1999 of a massive abdominal aneurism at the age of eighty-seven. Now, almost five years later, she reappeared.

Thoughts and emotions I did not immediately recognize crashed into my consciousness; thoughts of sorrow mixed with anger, joy mixed with fear and guilt, intense anxiety about my losses filled my heart. My thoughts frightened and unnerved me. But I had a distinct sense there was no turning back from this journey inward, revisiting old memories, seeking truth behind old myths, mourning losses and letting them go. I suspected my journey would require great courage.

Images of my mother invading my life splattered against the walls of my mind. Black and white photographic memories exploded into my consciousness, like pictures from an old family photo album. My body tensed as I fought to drive those memories back into the black hole from whence they came. But the flashbacks would not be denied.

First, I recalled a conversation that my sister-in-law initiated on my behalf. She said she knew how much I loved my mother, how she had personally witnessed my mother's possessiveness of her children, how she, my sister-in-law, believed that our friendship threatened Mother. "If we remain close friends, Janet, you will be caught in the middle and pay dearly. I think our relationship should be put on hold. For now, let's agree not to be friends," she cautioned. Her remarks were made shortly after I had moved from Connecticut to Pennsylvania, shortly after she and my brother had lost their six-year old son. I wanted desperately to remain close to them and to love and support them as well as I could. I was stunned by my sister-in-law's remarks and argued that I saw no reason I could not love both her and Mother.

Crashing into this memory came vivid images of my mother, as if possessed by demons, bursting into my bedroom early one morning, her eyes wild with anxiety and face crimson with rage accusing me of being a disloyal, underhanded daughter by "ganging up on her" with my sister-in-law. "In spite of your disloyalty, I will survive; I have always survived," she shouted, then slamming the bedroom door and stomping down the hall screaming "I will survive," she got in her car and drove away.

Memories of that traumatic encounter still resonate with the raw emotions I felt so many years ago. I can still feel myself lying in bed, shaking and sobbing, devastated by the attack from someone I considered my protector. My mother's face, filled with rage, kept flashing before my eyes. I remembered my sister-in-law's warning about the dangers our friendship posed to my well-being. I struggled to make sense of Mother's unprovoked outburst. *Could my mother's rage come from the notion that my sister-in-law had stolen her beloved son and now was stealing her daughter as well?* From somewhere deep inside, I felt a frighteningly dark question arising. *Was my mother's love unconditional as she had always told me, or was her love manipulative and self-serving?* My mother's tirade had left me feeling guilty, disloyal and depressed. I discussed Mother's outburst with my sister-in-law and we decided we would put our friendship on hold for the time being. I felt infuriated with Mother but nevertheless acquiesced to her demands. In time my fury turned to apathetic acceptance.

Another memory quickly emerged, seemingly disconnected. My daughter Susan, at age fifteen, had asked me after spending time alone visiting with my mother, whom all the grandchildren called by her initials, M.B., "Momma, why is it that every time I am with MB, she tells me how much she loves me, but every time I leave her house I feel so bad about myself?" Susan's comment made me realize that even MB's grandchildren were in some bizarre way perceived by her as threats or distractions. The matriarch seemed to always need the unlimited devotion of her children. Susan's question resonated in my heart. I too often left Mother's house feeling bad about myself.

As each memory surfaced, I added notations in my journal, hoping that the seemingly disconnected memories, like individual pieces of a giant jigsaw puzzle, would once connected, disclose a comprehensive picture.

Racked with these excruciating memories, new more insightful perspectives on old wounds emerged. Shards of etched glass that had been driven deeply into my soul began to melt into images of understanding. If I had not become so entrapped by her definitions of who I needed to be, how might my life have been different? "Why had I so passively accepted an identity defined by others?" I asked myself. Sheehy's notion of "the universality of inner guardian-dictators," as well as her assertion that most people spend their lifetimes struggling to free themselves, provided me with some insight into my passive acceptance of Mother's dominance.

Sweat began to trickle down my forehead, tears burned my eyes, and waves of nausea surged into my throat. I tried desperately not to think. *Suppress the infectious memories back into that black hole.* But I could not.

My mother always maintained that her marriage had been Camelot, the perfect marriage. She often said that whenever she and my dad had a disagreement they wrote love notes to each other to resolve whatever issues arose. At twenty-four and twenty-three years of age with two small daughters, Phil and I carried a lot of emotional baggage in the early years of our marriage. We did not write love notes to each other to resolve our issues. I often questioned how our marriage could have so many difficulties and be so different from my parents' marriage. Wasn't their marriage what marriage was supposed to be? Had we made a terrible mistake? Where was our Camelot?

As if some trap door had smashed open, memories emerged of my mother standing at the counter in a jewelry store where we had gone to buy Christmas presents, coldly staring at a woman at the other end of the counter. At forty years of age, I had never seen the woman before. I had never seen the look on my mother's face before, either. As the woman left, she and Mother exchanged an icy acknowledgment of each other. My mother remained unnerved.

When we got outside, I said, "Mother, who was that woman in the store?"

"I don't want to talk about it," she said.

"Well, I do," I replied. "I have never seen that particular body language from you before. I think I need to know what just happened in there. Who was that?"

She continued to look out the window on her side of the car. Her body remained rigid.

Instinctively, I knew I needed to push for an answer. "Mother, I am not going to start the car until you answer me. We'll just sit here until you answer my question."

Maintaining a dignified defiance, she relented. "It was a long time ago, when I was pregnant with Joyce," she said, continuing to look away from me. "I had worked for weeks making Halloween costumes for your dad and me and I was tickled with how wonderful the costumes turned out. Well, anyway, when we got to the country club dance, I stopped at a table to talk with some friends and when I turned around I couldn't find your dad in the crowded room. I thought maybe he had gone to the men's room, so I sat down at our reserved table and waited for him to return. When he didn't return, I went looking for him. I found him necking in a car in the parking lot with the woman you just saw in the jewelry store. I furiously demanded that he return to the dance. A short while later, I excused myself to go to the ladies room and when I returned he was gone. I found him necking with her again. I demanded that we go home immediately. It took many months for me to forgive him."

I burst into stunned laughter. "You have to be kidding me. Camelot destroyed! Good God, Mother, do you have any idea how much pressure your Camelot myth has put on my marriage? I'm sorry to laugh about what must have been an excruciatingly painful moment in your life, but I cannot reconcile the Camelot myth with what you are telling me. I must say, it puts my own fourteen-year marriage much more into perspective. You and I have often talked openly about the difficulties in my marriage. You could have so easily added some perspective to those difficulties if you had just been honest about your own."

"I never told anyone about it. I certainly never would have wanted you children to know this about your father. I wanted you to have beautiful memories of him."

I felt sad for my mother. I also felt sad for Phil and myself that the Camelot myth had lived for so long in the center of our marriage.

I added this memory to the other notations in my journal, convinced that journaling about each memory would eliminate the possibility that I might re-suppress them. It was time to determine who "me" is and what "me" would become for the rest of my life. I lay my journal on my lap and searched the blackness for a hint of the bay, the sight of which always strengthens my resolve. I could only hear it lapping in the distance.

All of a sudden I thought I heard footsteps on the bare wooden stairs. My heart raced, my head pounded, eyes wide and face frozen with fear. I dropped my pen and stared at the doorway that led to the top of the stairs. I could almost hear Mother shouting, "How dare you write negative things about me for the world to read. This is just another example of your disloyalty . . . disloyalty, even after I'm gone. Shame on you, Janet. I am so disappointed in you." I waited, frozen with fear, but she did not open the bedroom door.

I felt an enormous surge of guilt. *I loved and was loyal to you all my life,* I shouted inside my head. *I still love you Mother, always have, always will, but damn it, it's my time. I have to purge memories of our complicated relationship to free myself. I don't give a damn if you disapprove.* There was only silence. I sat immobilized and sweating. *What did you expect, Janet? Your mother is dead. She died five years ago at eighty-seven years of age.*

Squeezing my eyes closed, my head collapsed back against the cushions of the chair, a surge of great joy erupted from somewhere deep inside me. The joy was so intense it filled me with light. I'm quivering inside with joy, I thought. *My mother's death has created a safety zone from which I can confront our wounded relationship.* I also felt a sense of personal freedom I had never known: freedom to explore internal scar tissue to find me. Exhilarating joy mixed with twinges of guilt was indeed what I was feeling. *Her death has set me free to befriend who I wish, love who I wish, and even love myself more fully. Safe and free, Janet, no need to be defensive, no excuses or apologies needed.*

What the hell kind of a daughter am I, feeling joy following Mother's death?

Stop. You are not being disloyal. Searching through memories to recapture pieces of yourself is essential to your well-being. The negative power of Mother's voice has been stilled, so you can identify and grow your own voice. You can freely travel inward in pursuit of yourself, shedding prejudices, judgments, and perceptions that do not belong to you. You can travel deeply into yourself; confront honestly and openly your own darkness and light, with determination and without fear. For the first time in my life, that thought brought me face-to-face with the reality that I deeply loved, but also deeply feared my mother.

These startling memories had shaken loose insights about parts of me that I had never understood. Fears of success and failure, feelings of guilt and disloyalty, a driving need for approval and to please those around me, guilt for not measuring up to expectations, all left me open to emotional manipulation in my adult relationships. Over the years, I had honed my skills at reading others' facial expressions and body language, skills that were designed to ensure safety and non-confrontation. In some instances, the ability to read others' emotions proved helpful in developing strong intuition and empathy; other times it immobilized me, left me emotionally dependent on others' approval, and highly vulnerable to their manipulation.

Exhausted, I collapsed back onto my bed, knowing that sleep would come. As I drifted towards sleep, I reminded myself that examining the forces of darkness and light that inhabit us and those we love does not mean we dishonor or love them less. It does mean striving to live a more authentic life.

"Too many of us, like the subjects in
Hans Christian Andersen's story,
'The Emperor Has No Clothes' are watching
so many things go wrong, attentively listening
to so many lies and denying so many realities
simply because it is easier than taking up
the sword in defense of truth."

Renee Valentine

LANCASTER SUNDAY NEWS
LANCASTER, PA, 9/23/2007

CHAPTER NINE

TWENTY-FOURTH STREET MEMORIES

When I awakened the following day, thoughts of Mother and my childhood home filled my mind. I settled into my favorite padded reclining deck chair and inhaled the awesome beauty of the morning. A multitude of birds welcomed the new day from every tree top, while the bird bath's green clay frog spouted water onto his lily pad, creating soothing trickling sounds. The air felt cool against my skin but the rising sun held great promise for a warm, sunshine-filled day. I remembered a trip I made to my hometown, shortly before leaving Pennsylvania for the Cape . . .

━━━━►✕●─── ●

I had decided to dedicate a day to "talk" with my mother and revisit my childhood home in hopes of better understanding my internal legacy. After I dressed, I grabbed some breakfast, left a note for Phil and began the hour-long drive from Lancaster to Camp Hill, Pennsylvania. Lancaster city is surrounded by some of the most beautiful and fertile farm-

land in the world. Ribbons of verdant green and deep chocolate undulate in every direction while driving north on Route
283. I opened my sunroof to a canopy of cobalt blue sky and
felt the sun's warmth splash across my shoulders.

As usual on this stretch of road, I saw red-tailed hawks
soaring over fields searching for their breakfast. I pulled over to
the side of the road to watch, as a hawk with powerful wings
beating, suspended itself in flight. With magnificent grace and
deadly force, the hawk plummeted toward earth and scooped
up an unsuspecting rabbit in its razor-sharp talons. *Death has
no boundaries, no mercy, shows no preferences, it simply is an integral part of life. The hawk was doing what predators do, killing
prey to survive. I hope that the small rabbit did not see the hawk
before it struck. No pain, no fear, no waiting for death to arrive,
no false hopes that death will somehow be avoided.*

As I watched the rabbit writhing in the hawk's talons, a
memory tore into my consciousness—a memory of watching
another writhing rabbit die. I don't remember exactly, but at
about seven or eight years of age, I had decided to walk along
with my dad and brother on a hunting expedition behind
my grandfather's house. It was a beautiful sunny Sunday, and
as we walked the rolling green hills, we laughed and talked
about going swimming together later in the week. Suddenly,
both my dad and brother stopped short, raised their guns to
their shoulders and fired. In the distance, a small furry ball
splattered with blood dropped to the ground. Never having
been hunting before, I was totally unprepared for the violent
consequences. I dashed to pick up the rabbit and hugging it
to my chest, tore back to my grandfather's house sobbing,

"Hang on, little rabbit, hang on. I will save you." As my mother came running to meet me, I cried, "Help me, Mother, help me. We have to make the rabbit better. We have to save the rabbit. I promised him I would." Obviously, we could not. The rabbit's helplessness and vulnerability traumatized my heart and left behind a driving need to save all life's torn and bloodied rabbits.

I never went hunting again.

As I continued driving northward toward my childhood home, thoughts of my birth family kept me company. My sister Joan was three-and-a-half years older than I and my brother John, often referred to as my "Irish twin," was only thirteen months older; and my sister Joyce was three-and-a-half years younger. I found myself as the middle child in an Irish Catholic family in small town "1940s" America. My dad had been raised Irish Catholic. My mother, with a German Lutheran lineage, converted to Catholicism when she married my dad. My mother always said it was the easiest decision she ever made. From the first time she met him on a blind date, she knew that her heart belonged to "the most breathtakingly handsome man I had ever met."

At the outskirts of Camp Hill, my heart began to beat wildly. I felt compelled to revisit my mother's grave as I had done so often during recent months. Visiting my mother's grave meant revisiting my father's, my nephew's, and my stepfather's graves as well; so many losses, so much pain.

As the car passed through the cemetery's gray-stone entrance, I remembered that my maternal great-grandparents were buried near the entrance, a distance from the graves of my immediate family. I stopped, turned off the motor and walked from the road to my great-grandparents' grave site. Standing with my hand on the side of the obelisk-shaped gray-granite headstone, I thought about the many stories my grandmother Della told about her father, Martin Hench. She spoke of his role as an elder and choir member in the Lutheran church and his insistence that the family gather each evening so he could read scriptural passages. Della told me that he often prayed for the strength to gain control over his demonic temper. She remembered seeing him lose his temper, then in an act of repentance, drop to his knees, hang onto the edge of his wife's skirt and beg for forgiveness. My Grandmother Della's stories made it clear that my great-grandfather was a tormented man, a man she found difficult to forgive. Perhaps that was why she asked to have her ashes sprinkled in the stream near my family's farm, rather than be buried next to her parents.

My great-grandmother, Elizabeth Jane, having lived with my great grandfather for seventy-three years, must have found it in her heart to forgive him. At least I assume so, based on the longevity of their relationship. Martin died at ninety-one with Elizabeth holding his hand and singing him hymns. Elizabeth died at one-hundred-four, having lost her eyesight, but never having had any other serious health issues. She simply announced one evening that she was tired and was going to bed early. In the morning, my great-grandmother had died, her hands gently folded on top of her opened Bible.

—————◆×◆—————◆

Returning to the car, I drove deeper into the Camp Hill Cemetery to my immediate family's graves. I pulled the car over onto the grass at the side of the road, turned off the motor, and slowly walked towards the Brady headstone. As I drew closer to the light-gray marker, I saw my parents' names with birth and death dates carved into the headstone's foundation. Beside the main headstone were two small brass plaques embedded into the earth, one memorializing the birth and death of my six-year-old nephew, the other my step-grandfather's birth and death. I noted that there were flowers recently placed at the foot of Dad and Mother's headstone and I thought how pleased Mother would be that her family had not forgotten her. I wondered who had brought the flowers. The bouquet's deep red roses reminded me of the heart-shaped red roses that rested next to my father in his open casket. That memory made my eyes brim with tears and I began to sobbingly speak to my mother about missing her and the challenge I felt moving forward in my life without her. I sat down in the grass and between sobs updated her on all her children's and grandchildren's activities and travails, most particularly my older sister Joannie's treacherous walk with diabetes.

In my mind's eye, I pictured my family's final underground resting place; my father's casket large and bronze, my nephew's very small, white and fuzzy casket, and two small boxes holding the ashes of Mother and Tom, my stepfather. Containers designed to hold the most precious of family treasures.

Standing and looking out over all the headstones, thinking about the accumulated grief and loss of so many families across generations, I thought about death as the inevitable price of life. *Embracing death as just another part of life might integrate loss into our lives in a new way that could prove less painful.*

Resting on the nearby stone bench, I thought about God. I cannot help but wonder what God's role is in all of this? The Old Testament tells us of a wrathful God who punished humankind for disobeying his order not to eat from the Garden of Eden's wisdom tree. Is mortality His punishment? Is that what all this loss and suffering is about? Why wouldn't God have simply provided redemptive opportunities for His children so they might recover their presence in His garden? Or, maybe, God, you have. Is earth just another garden you have created, hoping that humankind will seek redemption through good decisions and deeds, earning our way back into your grace? Or could it be, God, that you do not have anything to do with death and dying?

I have often struggled to reconcile the wrathful, vindictive God of the Old Testament with the New Testament's God of love and forgiveness. During my young adulthood, I chose the loving God. As I matured, my struggle shifted to wondering if God might be merely a long-standing historical myth, used by generations to soothe their angst and suffering, to try to make sense out of the chaos of their lives. Could biblical scriptures be less about spiritual events and more about satisfying political realities and resolving the power struggles of their historical time? Was death merely our fragile bodies' natural biological response to environmental insults or genetic abnormalities, rather than God's wrath? Does God exist?

As I walked away from the gravesite, I was amazed at the solace found in talking with loved ones who had died, especially since a part of me did not believe they could hear me. *Maybe it's just a form of psychotherapy, talking yourself towards healing, acceptance and peace. Maybe it's believing there is an energy force with which we can communicate. Maybe it's just being unable to accept that loved ones, and ourselves, simply cease to exist. Maybe it's the ultimate human hope of a world beyond death and of a God who exists.*

Leaving the cemetery, I drove two blocks north to 24th Street and parked in front of my childhood home. The dark brown and white English Tudor façade had been painted a pale beige and a small addition had been added on the north side of the house. All else remained the same . . . the split rail fence . . . the formal gardens filled with pink and white peonies and purple irises that my sister Joan and I carried in every Memorial Day parade since we both could walk . . . the front living room window through which I imagined I could still see the huge Chinese ancestral scroll that hung on the living room wall.

In my eleven-year-old mindset, I entered the fairy-tale house. I felt as if I'd never left. My sister Joan had her own pale green bedroom at the front of the house on the second floor, which always seemed to radiate with sunshine. My brother John had his knotty-pine-paneled room in the center, filled with fishing poles, lures and BB guns. My sister Joyce and I shared a powder blue bedroom in the back of the house, which overlooked tall pines—the tall pines whose boughs touched the ground, creating magical backyard play spaces. Stairs led to a first-floor door, which when shut at night, softened the first-floor sounds and made us feel safe and snug in our second-floor bedrooms. Mother's nightly instructions to "get into bed immediately" were often ignored as we romped noisily over their heads. She sent Dad as the enforcer. Dad never failed to heavily rattle the door at the bottom of the stairs as he took off and snapped his leather belt. Fair warning, he was on his way. Gently, he always let us know when limits had been met. His Irish gentleness and wonderful sense of humor acted as a counterbalance to my mother's more-disciplined Germanic strengths.

Continuing reminiscences reverberated in my mind and heart . . . of my parents' first-floor bedroom's pink rose-covered wallpaper and silver-and-rose paneled doors that never failed to make me feel like I was entering a magic kingdom. I also recalled the childhood panic I felt when I awoke from a nightmare and had to make the long running trip down the dark stairs, through the large foyer and into my parents' bedroom. On perfect nights, Mother and Dad would let me stay all night snuggled between them, warm, protected, and loved. Sometimes I would even pretend I had had a nightmare just so I could recapture, as many times as possible, moments in the magic kingdom.

From my childhood perspective, we lived an idyllic life. My father, a successful dentist, and my mother, a dental hygienist turned full-time homemaker, created a home filled with laughter and love. Grandparents, as well as aunts and uncles, all contributed to a sense of permanency and safety that built a world where children could thrive. Some childhood experts say the middle child gets lost in the shuffle, but I always felt it to be a real advantage. My third-child-position and gender allowed me to avoid some of the pressures felt by my siblings. The first born, Joan, had to blaze a sibling trail through parental roadblocks; my brother, John, had to prove himself a man; and the youngest child, Joyce, struggled against always feeling left behind. Joyce often laughed saying, "I got what was left over in the gene pool, and was left behind by my siblings when they found their wings."

I had moved through childhood believing in fairies and magical kingdoms, talking with make-believe creatures, sliding down mud-slicked hills created by passing thunderstorms in the park across the street, damming up the park stream with the help of my siblings so we would have a "swimming hole," crawling into a storm sewer until reaching the manhole, which neighborhood kids had filled with comic books, small chairs and snacks. Catching fireflies and crayfish. Tenting with my "Irish twin" brother in the backyard as he told me spooky stories that inevitably always drove me inside to bed. Of feeling special when he invited me to pull his wagon full of fishing equipment to the creek if I promised not to talk too much.

I believed in Santa Claus until I was ten years old. I cried out in disbelief when an elementary school chum gave me the bad news. I ran home hoping to have Mother reassure me. The same friend told me where babies came from when I was twelve, and I didn't believe that story, either.

Santa Claus' death, in combination with the confusing and startling realization of how babies were created, were mere precursors of much more significant traumas to come, traumas that would shake my world to its core.

Easing out of the parking space at the front of the house, I drove around to the back of the house to the alley and six-car garage for another perspective. I wanted to get closer to the house without being too intrusive to the current occupants.

I passed our neighbor Izzy's house. Even after we had moved, Izzy remained a lifelong family friend—my mother's best friend, and, godmother to my daughter Tracy. I often played with her daughter's beautiful dolls and doll houses in a toy-filled room over their garage. Izzy would arrive with tea and cookies for our "ladies" tea party. These were enchanting times, somewhat like the magic contained in fairy tales minus the wicked witches and the fire-spewing dragons. As the sweet power of these memories resurfaced, I wondered how others survived life's witches and dragons having never had such a magical kingdom from which to pull their strength.

I drove down the alley and parked the car. I jumped out of the car and hugged the corner of the garage weeping. "I want this back, I want this back," I wailed aloud. I tiptoed around the garage so I could see the entire backyard and the area where John had always constructed his huts, a discreet spot next to the garage and hidden by tall hedges. I stood immobilized with the memories of helping John build his ramshackle huts. Huts he occupied on a daily basis, while I patiently stood outside waiting for an invitation to enter. I smiled, knowing that even if he never let me enter I would have happily helped him build his huts. I thought about how little had really changed in our relationship since our hut-building days. To this day, I still wait for his invitation and treasure any opportunity to spend time with him.

My mother and grandmother often told the story of my brotherly love and loyalty under fire. Once, John had jumped onto the back of a moving ice truck as it passed down the alley behind our house, fell off and sprained his ankle. Having been sworn to secrecy by John, I stalled when my mother lifted me up onto the end of the dining room table so she and my grandmother could maintain better eye contact while interrogating me. "John said he turned his ankle in a rut in the alley," Mother said. "Is that what you remember, Janet?" Repeatedly, she asked. I was only about five and lisped heavily which gave me a certain amount of cover. Finally, I blurted out that he had jumped on the back of the ice truck and fallen off into the rut. I quickly added that he should not be punished because his ankle was punishing him enough.

Thinking about the little boy in my lifelong favorite fairy tale, "The Emperor's New Clothes," and remembering that denying reality is easier than taking up the sword in defense of truth, I recalled feeling proud, but anxious, about stepping forward to tell the truth, but I couldn't help wondering at what cost. *Would my brother still love me? Would he be so angry with me that he would never again share his secrets with me? Had my telling the truth taught him that telling the truth was best and to think before he jumped?*

Tough choices then: speaking truth, modifying truth to avoid damaging others by revealing their secrets, or being politically correct and telling others what they want or need to hear. It ethically challenged me at five years of age; it has remained an ongoing ethical challenge throughout my life.

Emotionally exhausted, I rested my cheek against the corner of the garage and thought about all the times I had passed that corner with my dad. *Oh Dad, how I wish we could pass this corner just one more time together. There are so many things I want to talk with you about. You were gone before I had the time to really know you. I so desperately miss you. I want this magical kingdom back.*

Almost immediately, a vivid picture popped into my mind, a picture of my son-in-law hugging and kissing my two granddaughters, telling them of his love for them. Every time he so demonstrably shows his love to my granddaughters, my heart fills with affection for him, for I know that that demonstration of love goes directly into their hearts, lodges there and makes them whole. Tears of gratitude for his precious gift to my granddaughters, tears of pain thinking about the father's love I had lost at such an early age. Over the years I have often told myself that it was no big deal to lose my dad, many other folks had lost a lot more. But now, with a heart more willing to feel the pain of father loss and the vivid images of my son-in-law loving and confirming his daughters, I find myself struggling to free myself, conclusively, from the deep dark anguish-filled hole at my center.

On the drive home, I thought about magical Christmases, about selling lemonade on the corner, playing with our two beagle puppies, Jack and Jill, in a coal-tub filled with cool water, watching Joannie applying makeup at the dressing table in her bedroom and thinking she was the most beautiful and sophisticated sister anyone could ever have and dreaming of being just like her one day. I thought about my sister Joyce, who was the only sibling brought home from the hospital to that wonderful house, and how we had all struggled to adjust our familial standings to lovingly embrace this new baby sister.

As I drove south through the farmland on my return drive to Lancaster, I felt that I could almost hear my parents', grandparents' and neighbors' laughter as they played Canasta and drank beer late into the night. I wanted so desperately to hear that laughter again and to recapture innocence lost.

"We are broadened,
opened up to a new life;
the sea gives us back
to ourselves."

Susan St. John Rheault

CHAPTER TEN

LOBSTERS, SEAGULLS, AND OTHER CURIOUS MENTORS

*S*uddenly I realized I had been sitting in my deck chair for the entire morning with memories of visiting my mother's grave and 24th Street surging through my mind. After a morning immersed in internal landscapes, I felt it was time to rejoice in the external gifts of Cape Cod. I felt stunned that three weeks had already passed . . . so much to accomplish, so little time.

Striding across the deck, I grabbed my sunglasses and visor, stuffed some money into my shorts pocket and determined that I would quickly cover the mile-and-a-half walk to the restaurant by the harbor. Lobster salad, one of Scargo Cafe's specialties, was on my mind.

At the sheep farm, the farmer's wife was arranging more fresh flowers in vases under the umbrella table. I stopped momentarily to chat, mentioning that I hadn't seen as many gladioluses from her garden. She smiled and said, "The deer have ravaged our garden this year. We have the entire garden electrically fenced in, but they are so crafty. They figured out that they could jump over the gate, which is the only part of the garden not electrified. They ate our ripe vegetables and ravaged most of the gladioluses. My husband and I were bemoaning the loss of the glads because they are so labor intensive. We take them out of the ground each fall, dry and store the corms, and then replant them in the spring. When you have a half acre of them, it's a lot of backbreaking work. Alas, those clever animals outsmarted us. Now we have to figure out a way to outsmart them." I wished her well, thanked her for sharing her bounty, and as I walked away, she said, "Sharing our bounty with all God's creatures is sometimes very challenging." Indeed, I thought, indeed.

The walk from the sheep farm to the harbor is densely interspersed with pitch pines, hardwoods, flowering trees and shrubs, and abundant flower gardens. I passed meticulously landscaped properties surrounding colonial era homes as well as the newer faux mansions of the rich, designed to announce to the world that the owner is someone exceptionally accomplished. Some of these mansions are beautiful, some grotesque, but unfortunately they are transforming the genteel colonial ambiance and intentionally understated quiet charm of the Cape.

Passing the small park that overlooks the harbor, I paused to inhale the salty brined-filled air and sweet fragrances of flowerbeds bursting with color. I glanced at a brass plaque attached to a large rock that commemorates the mid-nineteenth century Shiverick Shipyard and those who built the last of the Dennis three-masted, square-rigged clipper ships and schooners that plied the world's waters. I tried to imagine one of those magnificent ships setting sail from the mouth of the harbor. I wondered if any whaling vessels had been built here.

As I continued my walk towards the café, I recalled some years earlier, overhearing folks at a nearby breakfast table talking about a whale that had beached itself near Corporation Beach. Phil, the girls and I never finished our pancakes and eggs. Corporation Beach is the public beach within walking distance of our cape house. We couldn't wait to see a whale up close. When we arrived, we saw an enormous gray mountain-like beast lying on its side. White-coated men and women crawled all over its dead carcass. We learned that the white-clad scientists had come from The Woods Hole Oceanographic Institute to determine what had killed the whale. Approaching the site, we quickly understood why most observers were standing upwind. The smell of rotting whale flesh overwhelmed us. Pinching our noses and breathing through our mouths, we quickly repositioned ourselves upwind.

Two of the scientists climbed the mountain-like gray mass and with a long swift thrust cut open the whale's body. Gigantic mounds of gooey intestines rolled out onto the sand. We watched for a couple hours, as the scientists extracted and bagged organ after organ from the whale's carcass. The remains were tied to the side of a boat and drug far out to sea and released. I knew that dying whales are sometimes accompanied close to shore by other members of their pod, all uttering sonar cries of despair. I wondered if its family was lingering nearby like humans awaiting their loved ones' body following an autopsy so they could properly say one more good-bye. I liked to think so.

Remembering the death of this magnificent animal brought sadness to my heart, but that sad memory triggered a celebratory memory, as well. Many years previously, Mother and my stepfather Tom, Phil, our daughters and myself had gone whale watching. As we stood listening to the guide talking about the intricacies of the whale's aquatic world, the loudspeaker suddenly shouted, "Mother and baby whale alongside." It's a wonder the boat didn't capsize as everyone rushed to the port side. There was a large Mother whale nursing a newborn calf. Everyone on the boat cheered with delight. Startled by the presence of the boat and human sounds, the baby disengaged from the Mother's teat and a cloud of white milk burst into the surrounding sea. Mother, with baby by her side, dove for the protective deeper water.

Thinking about the two whale sightings, I remembered Mother often saying, "I go before you to prepare the path. That is as it should be. Older folks must get out of the way so the earth's limited resources can be used to strengthen and support the young." Maybe, I thought, the older beached whale had simply decided it was his time and had said his good-byes and thrust himself onto the beach so that the Mother and her new calf could thrive. My eyes filled with tears as I thought about my mother's decision not to use preciously-needed health resources to prolong her own life. She had intentionally "beached" herself and had gone on before her children to prepare the path.

Simply confirmation of the circle of life, I thought.

At Scargo Café, I settled down at one of the picnic tables with my lobster salad sandwich, fries and an iced coffee and watched as a beautiful sail boat dropped its canvas in preparation for entering the harbor. I could overhear the skipper of a yacht talking to the attendant as she filled his gas tank, telling her of his plans to travel to Martha's Vineyard and Nantucket Island. Seagulls soared and squawked under an azure blue sky and half a dozen jet-black cormorants stood on top of rocks, wings spread in statuesque immobility, waiting for the wind to dry their feathers enough to make flight possible. I counted my blessings for being part of such an enchanting world.

My family and I had eaten breakfast or lunch at this restaurant a thousand times. The café is a small rustic shack surrounded by a boatyard, overlooking a pristine beach, and the marina's causeway. While sitting at outdoor brightly colored umbrella tables, eating fantastic, relatively inexpensive food, diners can watch sailboats, fishing and lobster boats coming and going from the harbor.

Walking towards the docks, I spotted an old friend about to motor into the bay to check his lobster pots. He shouted over the din of his engine, "Good morning, Janet. Care to ride along to check for hidden treasure?" I'd often observed these brightly colored lobster buoys bobbing in the bay like multicolored Christmas balls, as well as dissected and eaten hundreds of lobsters over the course of many summers. I developed a curiosity about these strange, delicious creatures. How could I possibly say no?

As we motored out of the harbor, I commented on the interesting perspective one got looking at the café from the water, rather than the other way around. "Yep," Bob shouted, "changing one's angle always challenges one's perspectives. Good thing to do from time to time. We're going to motor slowly so as not to create any wake in the channel, but when we get to the open bay, hold onto your visor. I like to clip along." Sure enough, when he hit the open water, he shifted the engine into full throttle.

Eventually slowing the boat Bob shouted, "I have six traps with half-red and half-white painted buoys in this general area, so if you spot red and white bobbing on the water, give a holler. Legally you can only pull up those buoys that match the distinct colors displayed on your boat. Men have been shot for messing with someone else's buoys." His voice startled me back into the moment

Just as I was about to shout, "I see a red and white buoy," Bob brought the boat to a stop alongside one of his traps. Pulling on the line attached to the buoy, he hauled the trap up onto the boat's railing. He quickly removed two trapped lobsters, threw the illegal "short" lobster back into the water, and efficiently banded the claws of the legal length lobster, and tossed it into his cooler. After he re-baited the trap with a piece of herring, reset the trap line and slid the trap back into the sea, we moved in search of the next buoy.

While harvesting each of his traps, Bob continued with the "Lobster 101" course to this neophyte.

"You must handle lobsters gently, banding them while holding them upright, because rough handling makes lobsters nervous, sometimes causing the animal to drop its claw. When a lobster throws a claw, it's usually to escape some dangerous situation, like rough handling by humans or even while doing battle with another lobster. Amazingly, given the chance, a lobster will regenerate lost appendages after its first molt. We band the legal length "keepers" claws just when we pull them from the traps to prevent their viselike claws from injuring each other. Makes it less likely that your fingers will be damaged as you unload them, too," he chuckled. "Not to mention that lobsters, not ordinarily cannibalistic in the wild, won't hesitate to use their claws to kill and eat one another if they find themselves in crowded conditions." As Bob lectured, I thought about the super-crowded grocery store storage tanks with banded lobsters pushing and shoving each other. Maybe, like lobsters, humans should be banded to keep them from destroying each other, I thought.

When the sun began lowering towards the horizon, we headed for home with six "keepers" on board. As we motored back to the harbor, Bob said, "Finding two legal-sized lobsters in a trap is considered a good day's catch. Each trap has a vent to allow smaller, illegal lobsters and other sea life to escape, and sometimes, even the legal sized larger lobsters somehow manage to back out of the vents. Then there's the matter of mending damaged lobster traps. Sometimes that chore feels like it's a full-time occupation," he laughed.

As I stepped from the boat, thanking Bob for a wonderful afternoon, he held out a lobster for me. Dinner! Feeling somewhat embarrassed, I was forced to tell him that I always paid to have my lobsters cooked and cracked, because I couldn't stand the sound of them clawing the inside of the pot as the boiling water overcame them. "Geez," I laughed, "and that was before I appreciated what adaptable and marvelously-wise creatures they are. Sort of gives you second thoughts about eating a creature that has worked so hard to survive under such adverse circumstances, only to be trapped and eaten by humans."

Bob laughed and exclaimed, "Think of it this way. Many creatures were created for our pleasure, but to spare you the agony of the boiling water, I'll drop off a cooked and cracked lobster at your house around six o'clock. You supply the melted butter. Does that fit in with your dinner plans?"

"Oh, I couldn't ask you to do that," I replied, hoping, of course, that he would insist. Happily, he did.

Sitting in the glow of candlelight looking out at the star-studded night sky with the lobster and melted butter at the ready, I raised my glass of wine to Bob's friendship and to the uniquely delicious creature who was about to share its bounty with me. As I pondered my newfound lobster knowledge, other questions arose: *How in the world do armored lobsters with huge claws mate? Does the female lobster lay her eggs and the male lobster fertilize the eggs outside her body as some fish do? Or is there some other magical adaptation required to overcome the handicap of armored bodies colliding? Well,* I thought, *rather than discuss the intimate sex life of lobsters with Bob, tomorrow I will have to do some independent research of my own.*

As I was preparing to retire for the night, Susan phoned. We talked about my sleepless encounter with Mother and the emergence of all those terrifying memories, about some of the memories elicited when I had revisited my childhood home, about insights garnered from the books I was reading. With her PhD degree in child psychology, Susan never fails to provide healing insights into my own struggles. She spoke about my mother's invasive and powerful personality and encouraged me to continue to explore this relationship. She quoted the adapted Biblical quotation on the brass plaque she had given me as

I left home: "Be still and know, Momma. Be still and know." We exchanged love and verbal hugs as we said goodnight.

The phone rang again. Phil laughingly asked who I was talking to for so long. We spoke about my previous evening's bizarre confrontation with Mother and how filled with insights that encounter had been. "I know your reflective journey is a difficult one," he said. "I just wanted to hear your voice and know that you are doing OK." I assured him that I was doing just fine, feeling painful emotions but making progress towards healing. "I find taking notes in my journal about insights, emotions, and issues I need to think more about, very helpful. After all, I only have myself to talk to." As we hung up, expressing love for each other, I thought about how lucky I was to be able to take this sabbatical from my family and to do so with their support and affection.

"I carry with me the remote aching of loss . . .
this is part of my identity that I can never change . . .
Our lives are shaped as much by those who leave us
as they are by those that stay."

Hope Edelman

CHAPTER ELEVEN

LOSS OF INNOCENCE

I awoke to the sounds of thunder and lightning, followed by a torrential downpour. Lightning lit up the sky and then disappeared into the bay. The sky to the northwest over Boston was jet black, promising the storm would be prolonged. I trotted downstairs, fixed myself a cup of chai tea, grabbed a biscotti, and ran back upstairs to watch the storm move east across the bay. Suddenly, as I lay snuggled protectively in my bed observing nature's awesome power, stormy childhood memories pushed their way into my awareness.

———————◆✕◆————————

In the spring of 1951, cancer crashed into our family's world. My fifty-year-old step-grandmother, whom my mother considered the sister she never had, had been diagnosed with uterine cancer. As I lay in bed at night, I could hear Mother and Dad talking about how devastated they felt, struggling with how best to support her through her ordeal. I could hear the fear in their voices.

Ironically, as my parents sat lamenting my step-grand-mother's cancer diagnosis, unknown to them, my dad's cancer was already invading his brain.

One gorgeous October day, six months after learning of my step-grandmother's illness, Dad shared with Mother, "Because of Florence's illness, I have tried to cope with my own discomfort without further burdening you, but as the pain in my head increases I can no longer remain silent, Martel. I need your help."

Mother immediately called a doctor friend and set up an appointment for the following day. After running some tests, Dr. Wilson referred him to a local neurologist, who in turn, referred my parents to Philadelphia Hospital.

Mother explained to us that Dad wasn't feeling well and needed to consult with a Philadelphia specialist to determine how best to relieve his discomfort. The next day, my grandmother, sisters, brother and I stood on the front porch waving to our smiling parents as they drove off shouting reminders to listen to our grandmother. Some days later, Mother called to tell us tests had revealed Dad had a brain tumor that required surgery. She planned to remain at the hospital until the surgery was over but would train home shortly afterwards.

Little did we suspect it was the beginning of a loss that would stay with us forever.

Two weeks later, Mother arrived home from Philadelphia to tell us that Dad had had the surgery. The tumor was malignant. She explained that the surgeons were only able to remove a portion of it since the tumor had invaded deep within his brain and any deeper surgical penetration would have killed him. Mother said Dad would be coming home in a few weeks and the doctors had told her in six months he would be gone.

Malignant. What is malignant? Cancer, the same disease that had attacked our step-grandmother? I can still see my mother reading to her four children from a bright yellow book about cancer, struggling to explain things she didn't understand and struggling to contain her own terror. I can still feel the hollowness, panic and need to scream, to shout that the doctors have to be wrong. I will pray to God and He will make it right. It must be a mistake. *Please God, please save my dad.*

***

Looking back now, from an adult's perspective, I can only imagine the questions my mother asked herself on the long train ride home alone. How do I tell my children that their father is going to die? How will I support them financially so we can remain together as a family? How will the five of us survive without Jack in our lives? How long does he really have? How much will he suffer? How will my spirit endure his loss? Who do I call for a job? How do I support Jack without having to tell him he's going to die? Why, dear God, why? I suspect she thought about how loneliness had plagued her and love eluded her until she met and married her "handsome Irish prince." How could it be that this forty-seven-year-old man in the prime of his life was to be taken from her after only seventeen years of marriage, the only really happy years of her life?

My dad came home from the hospital a few weeks later. My mother had arranged to have all of us stay with friends until she got Dad settled. I can still recall the fear and anxiety I felt as I walked home. As I crossed the front porch, I glanced in the living room window and saw Dad sitting in his favorite chair with his eyes closed and a huge bandage wrapped around his head. I retreated to the back door. My mother encouraged me to say hello. As I approached him, he opened his eyes and smiled, "Blondie, I'm so glad you're home. I like the four yellow roses on your pin. You look so pretty. I've missed you." Then he closed his eyes again. I ran to the foyer mirror to confirm for myself that there were only three roses on my pin. I shuddered, wondering if his vision had been impaired. I decided he had been joking with me as his way of trying to dispel the angst hanging in the air.

Dad had his bandages removed before Christmas to reveal an ugly scar, but at least it seemed to his children as if he were making some progress towards healing, towards life as it had been.

We celebrated the Christmas holiday during the day and individually roiled with fear and anxiety through the night when no one was looking. As a family, we never openly discussed his impending death, as if by not acknowledging it we might change the outcome or minimize our pain. It did neither.

After Christmas, Dad returned to work. He appeared to function as the dad we had always known. I began to tell myself that the doctors had been wrong, that they had gotten out the entire tumor after all. Surely this strong, handsome, loving man could not be dying. Dad's return to work was short-lived.

Mother spent the next three months tending to my father's needs, managing to secure a part-time job as a dental hygienist in the local school, traveling to New York with my step-grandmother for her cancer treatments and quietly laying the groundwork to sell my father's dental practice, sell our large home and find additional job opportunities to support her family. All the while, we continued to pray.

Within five months, Dad's weight had dropped from two-hundred and twenty pounds to eighty. He lost the capacity to walk and to see. During Mother's absences Joan and I, along with our grandmother, spent time helping Dad to the bathroom, encouraging him to eat and drink, doing whatever we could to support him during his desperate battle against a formidable foe. His deteriorating condition tore the last bit of hope from our hearts.

One spring day I came home from school and Daddy wasn't there. Mother had taken him by ambulance to the hospital to spare us the last few weeks. I begged Mother to take me to see him so I could say good-bye. Finally, against her better judgment, she took me to the hospital. I barely recognized him. When he opened his eyes, he did not recognize me. I ran out of the hospital and never had another chance to say good-bye.

Writing this sentence at sixty-four years of age still shatters my heart.

Dad's open-casket funeral still remains one of the most traumatic events in my life. Approaching his casket anticipating a sleep-like peacefulness, I looked into the bowels of hell. His emaciated body barely appeared to be connected to the grossly swollen head resting on a white satin pillow. My eyes immediately darted to the red rose heart propped against the inside of his casket. I never looked again. For years I was unable to go into a florist shop with its many flower smells and not be transported back to my father's funeral. To this day, I hate red roses. Death had shattered any remnant of childhood magic which remained. Childhood dreams had died in small pieces during the previous six months; the funeral itself completed the transformation of my world.

I wondered where God was.

After the funeral, I lay in my dark bedroom filled with terror, wondering if it were true that people who have died can reappear. I prayed that it was not so. I couldn't stand to see the tortured body of my father ever again. My cousin Pat shared my bed for a while, and that gave me some comfort. When my Aunt Betty called upstairs to say that it was time for Pat to go home, I wanted to scream, "No, she cannot go. I cannot be alone in the dark. Please, someone, hold me and make these nightmare images go away."

My father's funeral was the first time in my life I experienced true terror. It took years for the image of my dead father to fade and the image of the ebullient, rosy- cheeked, blue eyed Irishman to return.

Shortly after my father's death, my step-grandmother Florence was hospitalized because the cancer had returned. Mother visited with her every day. During one of the visits, Florence looked up and said, "Martel, promise me you will never again live with your father. He is an extremely difficult man. I love you very much. I want you to move on and find happiness again. Promise me. I do not want you to come back tomorrow.

I will not be here." Florence died during the night. The person my mother considered a sister, the second person in her life she had turned to for advice and loving support, was gone.

The death of my dad and step-grandmother shattered childhood perceptions of justice, mercy, courage, prayer, God, life and death. Most importantly, the losses created a fear that began to grow in my heart that there was no safe place to hide. Now I fully understood what the hunted rabbit in my grandfather's field must have felt as it frantically zig-zagged right to left, left to right, searching for safe cover. Instinctively, I knew that I would never experience life in the same way again. I began my lifetime quest to find someone, someplace, anything that would make me feel safe again. I found naïve solace in telling myself that our family had paid such an enormous price that we would not be asked for such a torturous sacrifice again.

My dad died in 1952 before the U.S. economy had fully recovered from the economic repercussions of the Depression and World War II. As siblings, we lay in bed at night in the weeks following the funeral hearing adults, including our parish priest, advising mother that the wisest course would be to put us into foster care until she could get on her feet. Panic rose in my heart until I heard Mother demonstrably reply, "Never. Not as long as I have a breath in my body. I will manage. I will scrub floors if need be. I will keep us together, somehow. I need time." An overwhelming sense of gratitude and thankfulness to my mother, mixed with fear that our family might be separated, emerged in my heart and drove deep into my being the understanding that my mother was my sole protector, my champion.

Mother sold our home, bought a small house which she restored and immediately sold for a profit, and purchased a slightly larger home which better served our family's needs. These initial real estate transactions began a series of buy, re-store, sell-at-a profit real estate deals which helped to supple-ment her income. My grandmother Della took care of us while Mother worked two part-time dental hygiene jobs. I vividly remember the day she told me that Mother could not live long under so much stress and that all of us should do all we could to take care of her. Having just lost our father, I wondered how we would survive without Mother. I pledged to myself that I would try to be whatever Mother needed me to be.

During this time, my mother shared with us pieces of her ordeal during Dad's Philadelphia hospital stay. "The surgeon arrived in the waiting room, looked at a woman sitting across from me, and said, 'Your husband has three months to live.' Then turning to me, said, 'And yours has six months.' The surgeon then turned and walked away. The next thing I knew I was clawing the side of a brick building blocks from the hos-pital. When I went back to see your father, he was stark naked, shackled to his hospital bed. He appeared deranged and tried to attack me. The nurses said it was a temporary reaction to the surgery and that he would stabilize." I was not able to dispel these images for years.

Mother also spoke of her stay with my dad's family in suburban Philadelphia while he was in the hospital. She always said their minimalist physical and emotional involvement ap-peared stoically uncaring and unsupportive. They never visited Dad while he was recuperating or offered to drive Mother back and forth to the hospital. Mother found it difficult to forgive them. As a result, we not only lost our dad, but following his funeral, lost all contact with our Irish paternal lineage.

Shortly after Dad's death, Mother ran for tax collector, having been told by our state senator whom she considered a good friend, that she had his support. He supported some-one else. She lost. During this time, my maternal grandfather, disoriented from the loss of his wife, found out he was being sued on a road construction job and risked losing his lifetime savings. For four years, while holding down two separate dental hygiene jobs, running for tax collector, selling my father's den-tal equipment and hiring and supervising an operator to run a beauty shop in my father's dental office, as well as parenting her four children, Mother also hired attorneys and bookkeepers in a desperate legal battle to save my grandfather's assets. It seems my grandfather, unable to read, oversaw the construction in the field and relied on his partner to take care of office matters. For four years, Mother and a bevy of attorneys fought the legal battles necessary to successfully settle the lawsuit that saved the bulk of my grandfather's savings.

Over the next few years, my mother established three beauty shops in three separate counties, became a stock bro-ker and bought, restored and resold real estate at a profit. She bought an apartment house, rented all sixteen units, saving one rent free for my grandmother. With my step-grandmother gone, she oversaw my grandfather's house as well.

Late at night I could hear her sobbing into her pillow. Her deep mourning was confined to private moments; not once do I ever remember her crying in front of her children, or discussing how she felt about the loss of our father. Mother's example of private mourning, of mourning alone, provided the model her children would follow. No adult attempted to help any of us children process our grief. We simply moved on as a family, with each individual member managing as best he or she could.

Mother, striving to financially provide for her family and mourning the loss of her husband and stepmother, lacked the emotional resources to adequately cope with the differing emotional needs of her children—Joan seventeen, John fourteen, myself thirteen, and Joyce nine. We began to separately move among our differing peer groups, desperately trying to right ourselves. Mother, attempting to right herself as well, began to date, further complicating her children's adjustments to their new reality.

Joan, while struggling academically, had to take on many adult responsibilities while Mother worked. She got a part-time job working in a local department store to cover some of her own costs and began to date the man she would eventually marry. Emotionally, Joan had not only lost her dad, her champion, but found herself engaged in an intense effort to hold onto herself in the face of Mother's dominant and very different personality. Joan matched her strong will and stoicism against Mother's. There were losses and gains on both sides, with each woman eventually retreating to her own corner, accepting a draw.

John also struggled in school but excelled at sports. He tried to move from childhood to manhood in a household filled with women. Not only did he have a mother and three sisters to contend with, he was surrounded by my grandmother and all her female friends, who spent many evenings around our dining room table trying to support Mother through her ordeal. With the loss of his male role model, John retreated into male-dominated activities. To this day, he still prefers the company of men.

Joyce, who excelled in school, continued to share a bedroom with Mother, since John needed his own room, and Joan and I shared the third small bedroom. Joyce spent time alone with Mother, while her adolescent sisters and brother, attempting to quell the pain and right themselves, turned to their peers for comfort. I suspect that Joyce's youthful vulnerabilities exposed her more intensely to Mother's mourning. Joyce's bonds with Mother were the strongest of the four children and remained that way until Mother's death.

At school I did what I had to do academically to get by without embarrassing myself. In seventh grade, at age twelve, I matured early and became extremely self-conscious. I decided walking around with my shoulders hunched was the best approach. I remember my math teacher, who was also the high school football coach, calling me to the board to solve a math problem. I could not solve it. As I struggled at the chalkboard he announced to the class, "Don't worry, Miss Brady, with a body like yours you won't have to worry about math. Some man will be happy to take care of you." I slinked back to my seat, feeling such mortification that I have never forgotten the incident. To this day, 52 years later, I can still feel the humiliation I felt so long ago.

The summer following seventh grade, at age thirteen, I

fell in love with a high school junior, almost four years my senior. Class President, football captain, basketball captain, and
track star, the essence of tall, dark and handsome. Like a prince
from one of my magical childhood fairy tales, I believed he
had ridden into my life to make the damsel whole again. For
two years, we spent every moment together, pledging to marry
when he graduated from college. He left for Brown University,
Providence, Rhode Island, in the fall of 1955. We wrote to
each other almost every day. I visited Brown for a long college weekend in the fall of 1956; I was a sixteen-year-old high
school sophomore, who had never been on a college campus
or for that matter out of Pennsylvania. On the train alone, I
remember feeling anxious about how I would relate to him on
an entirely different playing field. Everyone had told me it was
unrealistic to believe our relationship would continue once he
went off to college. As I looked out of the train window at the
beautiful New England countryside, the lyrics "they tried to tell
us we're too young, too young to really be in love" resonated
in my heart. Still acutely missing the loss of my father's love, I
wondered if I could survive another overwhelming loss? I wondered how one prepares her heart for such an eventuality.

That evening, as I sat on the bottom step of the staircase
at my first fraternity party, a young woman sat down next to
me, introduced herself, and told me that she had tried repeatedly to get Ed to date. Ed had always explained to her that he
did not date at college because he had someone very special at
home. While she spoke, I thought, maybe the cynics are wrong
about our age differences dooming our relationship. Maybe we
will beat the odds? I slept at a local guest house and spent most

of the weekend trying to make sense of fraternity house parties that never seemed to end. We attended a football game, stole some quiet time together walking around town and down by the river, but I felt distanced from him. On my way back to Pennsylvania, I was saddened, confused and anxious.

I began to think more about what others called the inevitability of time, distance, and differences in our ages and worried that if, over time, they proved right, I would have sacrificed all the fun activities of my senior high school years. I told myself that I would begin to date others, but remain faithful to Ed in my heart. Naively, I thought faithfulness in my heart would suffice.

When a buddy of Ed's told him I was dating others, Ed apparently felt I had broken my word to him. In our correspondence, I confirmed I was dating others, but that he remained my love. Christmas 1957, having just arrived home for the holidays, he called my girlfriend's house where I was visiting. He said he was on his way downtown and wanted to talk with me and give me the suede jacket he had gotten me for Christmas. He asked me to meet him outside.

I felt anxious and afraid, recognizing the distanced formality in his voice. I was confused too by the strange venue he chose to give me my Christmas present. I consoled myself by thinking that if anything was really amiss, he wouldn't have bothered to give me a Christmas present at all. As I stood outside waiting for him to arrive, I couldn't shake my uneasy feelings. My heart beat wildly when he walked across the front lawn and handed me a large box. I explained that I didn't realize I was going to see him, so the monogrammed cigarette lighter I had for him was at home. There was no response to my comment. When I looked into his eyes I felt total panic. I wanted to run, screaming, "I love you. I really do. Don't do this." Instead I stood in stunned silence as he broke off our relationship.

I still remember standing mutely watching his back, clad in a dark green silk shirt with white diamond-shaped figures, fade into the darkness. I wanted to die. Was it because I had dated others? Was it merely the inevitable toll of distance and difference in our ages? Was it that he really never loved me? Those torturous questions would burden my heart for years to come. Cursed by pride and inhibited by shyness, I never found the courage to tell him how I felt or to ask him why.

My feelings of loss were compounded by the painful loss of my father, and those combined losses lodged so completely in my heart that it took most of my adult life to shake them loose. As my sister Joyce said, "There is a part of me that wishes you had never met him. He altered the course of your life and life's choices. He cost you dearly, Janet."

"I know, Joycie, I know," I replied. "But, I have come to understand that most of us struggle to repair ourselves when first love dies. Moreover, most of us would not be willing to sacrifice the memories to avoid the pain. Unfortunately, my struggle to right myself was compounded by the fact that it was so close to Dad's death."

Now, these many years later, I understand that as a young woman I was looking desperately for someone to fill my wounded spaces, looking for someone to love and someone to love me. Someone who would keep me safe. I grew my mystical

notion that my perfect prince would not permanently disappear as my father had done, but would ultimately ride back
into my life, place a magic kiss upon my lips to heal all my
wounds, and we would live happily ever after.

* ——————✦✕✦—————— *

As I write this, I reflect again on Sheehy's premise that in
order to move forward developmentally, we must be willing
to give up magical thinking. Sheehy and my sister were correct: the myth of the perfect prince was just that, a myth. The
prince never had to stand the test of time. My prince stole my
innocence and childhood carefree learning and exploration. He
left behind untold scars and sorrow that merged with the deeply painful scars left by the death of my father. My underlying
struggle to reconcile the fairy-tale myth of the perfect prince
with the realities of Phil and my marital difficulties cost both
Phil and me dearly.

Just as suddenly as the morning's sky had darkened with
the approaching thunderstorm, the beautiful cobalt blue sky
reemerged, as if to startle me out of my dark ruminations. The
golden sunshine shafting through my bedroom window beckoned me back into the light. As I dressed for the day, I thought
about yesterday's lobster discussion with Bob. I had promised
myself that I would find out how lobsters mate, so I decided
to devote the morning to internet research. Grabbing a quick
juice and toast breakfast, I began my search for the myster-
ies of lobster love. At www.gma.org/lobsters, Dr. Jelle Atema
of the Marine Biological Laboratory, who has studied lobster

mating behavior for twenty years, claims lobsters make tender lovers. The idea that someone would spend years studying lobsters mating and claim lobsters make tender lovers left me belly laughing breathlessly.

Dr. Atema tells us that a female lobster can mate only just after she sheds her shell. Lobster society has evolved a complex, touching courtship ritual that protects the female when she is most vulnerable. When she is ready to molt, the female approaches a male's den and wafts a sex "perfume" called a pheromone in his direction. The female lobster does the choosing. She usually seeks out the largest male in the neighborhood and stands outside his den, releasing her scent in a stream of urine from openings just below her antennae.

He responds by fanning the water with his swimmerets, permeating his apartment with her scent and emerges from his den with his claws raised aggressively. She responds with a brief boxing match or by turning away. Either attitude seems to work to curb the male's aggression. The female raises her claws and places them on his head to let him know she is ready to mate. They enter the den, and some time after, from a few hours to several days later, the female molts. At this point the male could mate with her or eat her, but he invariably does the noble thing. He gently turns her limp body over onto her back with his walking legs and his mouth parts, being careful not to tear her soft flesh.

They mate "with a poignant gentleness that is almost human," observes Dr. Atema. The male, who remains hard-shelled, inserts his first pair of swimmerets, which are rigid and grooved, and passes his sperm into a receptacle in the female's body, where the sperm will remain viable for at least nine months, until she spawns. She stays in the safety of his den for about a week until her new shell hardens. By then the attraction has passed, and the couple part with hardly a backward glance.

During spawning, the eggs flow from openings in the female's body over the receptacle where the sperm is stored, thus fertilizing the eggs. The fertilized eggs attach to the mother's swimmerets with a natural adhesive. They remain protected and aerated throughout an incubation period of ten to eleven months, at which point she lays her eggs. The number of eggs she lays depends upon her size. Female lobsters carrying eggs are known as "berried" lobsters.

I struggled to picture a large hard-shelled, multi-legged, large-clawed male "tenderly" using his rigid, grooved swimmerets to impregnate this vulnerable soft-bodied female. I was intrigued by the notion that the female lobster selects her mate and uses her perfumed scent to lure the male from his den. I also wondered how many times the male's desire to eat overwhelms his desire to mate! The female selects and lures. The male mounts and impregnates; the female is left to incubate the eggs for ten to eleven months and then finds herself alone through the birthing process and the protective responsibilities of her young. Hmmmm. Sounds vaguely familiar, I speculated—alone during the birthing process and mostly alone parenting the offspring. I felt a sense of sisterhood with this strange creature.

" . . . our own wounds can be vehicles
for exploring our essential nature,
revealing the deepest textures
of our heart and soul,
if only we will sit with them,
open ourselves to the pain . . .
without holding back, without blame."

Wayne Muller | LEGACY OF THE HEART

CHAPTER TWELVE

BREAKING DOWN FENCES

*N*ow that I had satisfied my curiosity about the lobster's tender love making, I pulled another book from my desk, and settled down on the deck with Nancy Friday's *My Mother/Myself: A Daughter's Search for Identity.*

The sky was so clear and the air so crisp that I could see the entire way across the bay to Pilgrim's Monument in Provincetown, a fist-like appendage at the end of the Cape's "arm." Our house is in the crick of the Cape's elbow, so on clear days we can sit on our deck and look directly across the bay to Provincetown. I marvel at the tenacity of this sixty-five-mile long shifting, moaning, adapting sandbox that refuses to yield to the ravenous tides, hurricane strength winds, excessive development and the onslaught of thousands of year-round residents and summer vacationers. Looking out over the deserted cranberry bog and beyond to the magnificent sparkling bay, I said a silent prayer that this island's delicate ecosystem could continue to adapt and adjust against overwhelming insults.

Black-capped chickadees, sparrows, and finches, all pushing and shoving for the best perch covered, the backyard feeder. I watched in sheer delight as my favorite bird, a male American goldfinch, announced his arrival to our bird bath with a high-pitched per-chik-o-ree. His small exquisitely brilliant yellow body, with crisply distinguishable black and white wings, a notched tail and a black cap, quivered in anticipation of an afternoon shower under the stream of water arching from the mouth of the birdbath's clay frog. Having gorged himself at our thistle feeder, he showered, shimmying and shaking under the cool stream of water, and hopped up on the edge of the birdbath, leaned forward to fill his stubby bill with water, then tipped his head skyward. He repeated the filling and tipping action until he was seemingly satisfied. Amazingly, this tiny bird, landing just inches from where I sat, showed no signs of fear or intimidation at my presence. As if to say thanks, he tipped his tiny head in my direction and then quickly flew, in classic finch roller coaster ups-and-downs, into the cranberry bog.

I watched a gray squirrel approach a metal squirrel baffle attached to the bird feeder's pole, a baffle designed to prevent squirrels from gorging themselves on bird seed. I chuckled. Will this be his lucky day? Every day, squirrels test themselves against the baffle. It never fails to evoke belly laughter from anyone lucky enough to be on the deck to observe their antics. Today was no exception. A squirrel demonstrating its unbelievable dexterity shimmied up the pole, its tail flicking in anticipation, banged its head against the baffle, stopped, backed down the pole a bit, ran at the baffle, and banged its head again. Appearing to consider its dilemma, it revised its technique a bit by repositioning its tiny paws, lunged at the baffle with greater speed, only to bang its head even more severely. It hung on the pole, continuing to bang and revise, and finally, with a look of disbelief on its tiny face, slid down the pole and scampered off. Each time I observe this ritual, I can't help giggling about all the times I have approached life the same way. Bang, revise, bang, revise.

I opened Nancy Friday's book suspecting that it might challenge many of my deeply-held beliefs about motherhood generally and my mother-daughter relationship in particular. I was unprepared for the seismic bedrock shift upon which I had so confidently built the relationship with my mother.

Friday comforts those of us who, as adults, still struggle with parental separation issues by telling us that the process of separation from parents is lifelong. I certainly know that to be so. Friday reassures readers that most parents do the best job they can under their particular circumstances and do not mislead nor consciously and intentionally damage their children. I thought about Mother's extremely challenging childhood. She had to parent herself. I marveled that she had any constructive parenting skills.

After Mother's death, as I began to examine the realities of our relationship, an overwhelming sense of fear and guilt began to surface—fear that I was releasing long-suppressed memories that would undermine my love for her. I wanted desperately to continue to love her. But memories surfaced that made it clear that my mother had not loved me unconditionally, as she had always claimed . . . and as I had always believed. Those memories insisted I understand that she had not loved me perfectly, that she had used manipulation, blackmail, possessiveness, jealousy, anger, anxiety, guilt, and even rejection to remain in control of what she believed rightfully belonged to her.

Friday said that all parents do the best they can. *So, holding onto the notion of a perfect unconditional love is counter-productive if I am to see my mother clearly. After all, I am not perfect. I have not parented perfectly. I want my children to love me in spite of my conditional parenting. I had done the best that I could. I suspect Mother had done likewise.*

I mentally thanked Nancy Friday for helping me to accept that parents love imperfectly and that even though many of us are raised to believe mothers love their children perfectly, many times they actually love ambivalently. I felt some of the intensity of my mother-daughter struggle dissipate into the air.

I still needed to examine the acute sense of guilt I felt whenever I challenged my mother. Even now after her death, my guilt about probing our relationship had intensified, threatening to distort, if not end, my search for self. Somewhere deep inside I knew that if I should die without discovering who I am, it would be like never having been born at all.

Suddenly, I heard an unfamiliar almost bee-like buzzing sound next to my chair. I turned towards the flower baskets filled with deep purple petunias and eyed a tiny flying jewel, an iridescent green, black and red hummingbird with wings beating so rapidly they appeared to be an indistinguishable blur. My mind immediately revised its thinking to note that I had not one, but two favorite birds: the American goldfinch and the smallest of all North American birds, the ruby-throated hummingbird, the only hummingbird out of three hundred twenty-five species which is common in the East.

His bright red throat identified him as male. As he hovered with upright wings beating, using his long slender bill and tongue to sip nectar from a deep-hued purple petunia in the flower basket just above my head, I marveled at his rainbow-like iridescence caused not by feather pigmentation, but rather by the arrangement of his feathers in relationship to the light.

The hummingbird is the most skillful flyer of all birds, with the ability to take flight at high speeds, stop in an instant, hover in the air, and fly backward, (the only bird with this capacity) forward, and sideways. Because hummingbirds fly so much, they have poorly-developed feet, allowing them to perch but barely walk. His tiny feet make him lighter and a more efficient flyer. He can hibernate overnight by lowering his body temperature, ruffling his feathers to increase insulation against the cold, and assume dormancy, allowing him to conserve energy as he rests.

This amazingly miraculous small creature has the capacity to migrate distances of 2,500 miles. As I softly whispered, "Tiny, little man, you are truly a magical spirit," he hung suspended in the air, looked at me, and at breakneck speed shifted into reverse, darting effortlessly backward, as if showing off his spectacular flying skills. I shouted to him, "I will think of your tiny being flying thousands of migratory miles against all the odds the next time I face circumstances that seem overwhelmingly impossible, little man. Thank you for reminding me that nothing is impossible."

My thoughts returned to Mother. *Did she love me? She had repeatedly said so all my life. Had I felt unloved, manipulated and intimidated when we crossed swords? Yes. How could I say she had loved me enough to give me a self, when I am currently struggling to determine who I am? If she had given me a self, why would I have suffered from homesickness every time I was separated from her? Could my homesickness have been driven by an insecurity created when my dad died? Or, could the chaos and severity of my mother's life have prevented her from seeing her children as separate selves, leading her to consider her children as mere extensions of herself? If she had parented her children as mere extensions of herself, the symbiotic relationship all her adult children had with her was understandable.* Yet, Friday asserts that symbiosis after the age of three is unhealthy.

Love implies separation! Symbiosis and real love are mutually exclusive. As I added those thoughts to my journal, I felt a profound shift somewhere deep inside myself as I struggled to integrate this totally foreign notion.

It's the roots and wings thing, I thought. *In some ways it's even more complicated than that. It doesn't just mean loving children the way you choose to throughout their formative years and then giving them their adult wings. I think it means loving them profoundly throughout their lifetime with an ongoing and deep commitment to their uniqueness and separateness.*

I smiled, thinking about my own mother's inability to see her children's separateness and I felt twinges of guilt that I too had often failed to honor my own daughters' uniqueness as well. *I suspect parents often create assumptions about their right to impose what is considered to be appropriate for the good of the child, even long after the child has become an adult. Children merely pass through their parents on their way to becoming who they need to be, not who the parents need them to be. This parental understanding is vital to the well-being of children.*

Certainly that was not something my mother understood when I was young. In adulthood, I continuously struggled with how best to satisfy her emotional needs for symbiosis. Mother had body language and a 'Little Red Hen' tone of voice which never failed to remind her children they had strayed too far and thus were neglecting or displeasing her. I dreaded that tone of voice because I knew from past experiences it elicited a sense of despair, guilt and anger. I felt I needed to accommodate her emotional needs, but my feelings of being manipulated inevitably led to feelings of resentment followed by guilt. The most destructive force in this symbiotic dance between my mother and me was the feeling of guilt that lodged deep inside me and distorted my ability to hear my own voice.

"Janet," I would say to myself, "she has been a wonderful, sacrificing, caring Mother; you owe her your loyalty and attention. She has had a long and arduous struggle all her life. What kind of daughter are you?" I never failed at attempts to assuage my guilt by doing my mother's bidding, hoping that maybe this time her terrifying loneliness would relent and she would cease needing to live through me.

I began to realize that the source of my guilt was my mother's symbiotic parent-child expectations. No wonder she fought so hard when she felt we had strayed from her. In her mind, she was losing a part of herself. In a letter I discovered addressed to her adult children after she died, she wrote, "My children have gone on, and that is as it should be." I like to think that, at eighty-seven years old, my mother had finally come to understand that adult children separate, but still continue to love you.

Dusk had fallen over the deck and as the multitude of birds rushed about taking their last bit of sustenance before retiring for the night, I poured myself a glass of chardonnay and settled on the deck to watch the sun descend into the sea. There was a disquieting silence. I realized that all the small birds had disappeared. A predator had to be near at hand! On the railroad tie wall, which ran along our neighbor's yard very near the bird feeder, sat a huge red-tailed hawk. All the birds had disappeared into a small lollipop-shaped bush where they crouched in as much silence as their fear and panic would permit.

A giant red-tailed hawk perched regally, with razor-sharp talons extended over the edge of the railroad ties. Using his fierce intelligence in an attempt to outwit his prey, his brilliant yellow eyes were keenly focused on the bush, never moving. Losing patience after ten minutes, he suddenly flapped and feinted, landing on top of the bush, talons extended. A bevy of small birds shrieked in fear and confusion, but continued to cluster together within the depths of the bush. The hawk fluttered his enormous wings, repositioned himself and inserted his huge beak and steely yellow eyes into the top of the bush, hoping that sheer terror rather than surprise would force one of them to make a mistake. If one of the small bird's terror overwhelmed it and it flew from the bush, the hawk would snatch it in flight with his talon's hooks, puncturing the bird's soft tissues until death.

I could no longer stand the tension. Jumping to my feet, I shouted at him, "Stop your intimidation, you big lug. Catch them in the air if you must, but stop terrorizing them." Looking disdainfully at me over his shoulder as if to say, "Lady, I am a predator. What don't you get?" he flew away. I laughed out loud, as the lollipop bush slowly came to life. A gaggle of tiny multicolored heads popped out of the bush, creating an almost decorated Christmas-"tree-like"-magic. After a few moments, having overcome their terror, the birds returned to the feeder to resume eating before retiring into the safety of the large trees for the night.

As darkness descended over the Cape and I watched the burnt orange sun disappear into the black sea, I thought about the relationship of power to vulnerability: hawk to prey, parent to child.

During dinner preparation, my thoughts returned to my mother who often spoke of her overwhelming sense of loneliness and her determination to convince my dad that they should have four children, not just two, as he would have preferred. Mother spoke often telling us how beautiful we were in comparison to her friends' children, how fulfilled and happy she felt to be a mother. I wondered if Mother's glorification of motherhood, the tendency to present an image of her perfect love for us, stemmed from the damage done by her own mother's imperfect love. Mother may have felt she had to present an image of perfect love because her own mother's love had been so destructive and self-serving.

Most likely, Mother's sense of overwhelming loneliness and distrust of her parents drove her to create myths. She had loved me well enough that I grew up feeling loved, imperfect or not, and her love had allowed me to grow enough inner strength to undertake this odyssey in search of self. *She did indeed do the best she could,* I thought. *That is all we can ask of those who love us.*

Returning to the deck, I stood watching the stars emerge from the night sky and thought about the powerful messages that had been stored within my heart. Nancy Friday called them *illusions.* Gail Sheehy called them *magical thinking.* Both agreed that these childhood survival tactics had to be recognized and given up if we are to maturate and become all we can become.

Thinking about Friday's assertions "to take a mother's words about love at face value is to distort the rest of our lives in an effort to find again this ideal relationship," I realized that deeply stored illusions had prevented me from hearing my own voice. I wondered how deeply I had internalized my mother's notion of idealized love and how it might have distorted my marital expectations. The symbiotic expectations within my birth family most surely have been carried into my marital and parenting relationships.

I heard my mother's voice saying, "You are my life. If I didn't have you children after your father died, I would have perished. I love you more than life itself." Mother's love deeply affected her children, consistently defining who she needed us to be and corralling us with obligatory fences, which ensured that she would have both physical and emotional accessibility whenever needed.

Considering the height and strength of my corral's fence, I was initially stunned when Friday challenged me with the notion that not only is it appropriate, but essential to a daughter's growth and well-being to realistically examine the love between her mother and herself. But as I intensified the examination of my personal mother-daughter relationship, I felt a sense of exuberant joy. I was creating a space for me. I realized my entrapment had been so complete I was held captive in a place that was not me. It never occurred to me that I had the strength and tenacity to jump the fence to freedom and survive. "That is why I have not been able to find myself, hear my own voice," I shouted out loud.

I could hear my mother's voice in Friday's analysis, "Believe that I love you no matter what I say or do to you . . . No one will ever love you as I do. Mother loves you best in all the world and I will always be there for you . . . many mothers offer this kind of impossible love because they are lonely and want to bind their children to them forever." And I could hear my own voice as well. I know that during the difficult years of my own marriage, when I felt so alone, I, too, projected perfect love to my own daughters, hoping it would bind them to me forever. But, I had experienced mother-daughter symbiosis and knew the cost.

As Phil's and my marriage healed and became more spiritually nurturing, I slowly became more capable of loving my daughters with less binding constraints. It was a lot easier for me to take down my daughters' "corrals." For my mother, her children were her only refuge from a torturous sense of loneliness.

Did I not have to take some responsibility for having internalized Mother's tangled-up notion of love? I had projected her notion of perfect love onto all my other relationships at some peril to myself and those around me. Should I not have been capable of distinguishing myth from reality and had the emotional courage to see, as Sheehy tells us, "Honest love admits errors, hesitations, and human failings; it can be tested and repaired?" I am most fortunate that my marriage, "tested and repaired" many times over, survived my mother's projection of her perfect marriage.

Friday suggests that love between a mother and a daughter is not so sacrosanct that it cannot be questioned. In actuality it must be questioned if one is to find "a resting place on which to build oneself." This resonated in my very core. I grabbed my journal from the bedside table and wrote, "mother-daughter love not sacrosanct, must look at relationship realistically if you are ever to find yourself" Friday was telling me that my probing was long overdue, and for that encouragement I was deeply grateful.

My greatest fear had been addressed. I could safely peel away all the layers of illusory maternal perfection and still deeply love my mother. I could forgive myself, as well, for not loving my daughters perfectly. I could forgive Phil for not being able to love me or our daughters perfectly. As that transformative notion pushed into my soul, I felt the overwhelming sense of guilt I had carried like an albatross around my neck take flight.

Listening to the rhythmic sound of waves lapping at the shore, I drifted towards sleep filled with a sense of peace I had never known.

"Woman must come of age by herself . . . learn to stand alone. She must find her true center alone."

Anne Morrow Lindbergh
GIFTS FROM THE SEA, p.90

CHAPTER THIRTEEN

EXPANDING HORIZONS

When I awakened in the morning, I heard an unfamiliar sound. I ran to the window and watched in amazement as a mother red fox sat silently at the back of our yard observing her three small pups rolling around on top of one another, yipping in sheer delight. I ran downstairs, quietly opened the sliders and crawled across the deck on my hands and knees to get a closer look. Ever vigilant for potential threats to her pups, her head turned in my direction, and I froze. I observed her scanning the yard and the sky to ensure that her babies were safe. As she began running for the high brush, her tail positioned horizontally like a ship's rudder, I broke into laughter as she called her pups to follow. *Mothers are ever vigilant protectors when their babies are young. Nancy Friday would be most pleased that the mother fox had symbiotically attached to her babies,* I thought. *I'd have to wait for their return to see if mother fox gives her babies wings,* I mused.

Maybe it was the sighting of the mother fox or maybe it was the thought of my own struggle to sort out the com-

plexities of the parent-child relationship that caused unbidden
memories of prep school and college to surge into my mind.

———✕———

Back then, recoiling from the back-to-back losses of my
father and first love, as well as struggling with all the normal
adolescent baggage, I began to run hard and fast, challenging
anything and everyone who got in my way. For the first time in
our lives, Mother and I began open warfare. She had approved of
Ed, but strongly disapproved of my new boyfriend choices. I did
not care. I was determined to make some of my own choices; she
was equally determined that I would not. Mother was horrified
that I was dating someone she said was "from the wrong side of
the tracks." I declared there wasn't any wrong side of the tracks,
and that I should be able to make my own choices. We fought
daily and the tension escalated between us.

One evening as I was dressing to go out, we literally came
to physical blows. She grabbed and shoved me back onto my
bed saying I was not leaving the house, and when she moved
towards me the second time I kicked her. Unfortunately, my
kick landed on her abdomen, which was healing from a recent hysterectomy. The encounter shocked us both. No real
harm was done except to my psyche and hers. Not long after
that fight, she and I decided the best course for my senior year
was to go away to boarding school. I would be removed from
current bad influences and be exposed to a whole new world
of learning and opportunity. Hopefully, I would be distracted
from the loss of my first love.

I never felt as lost and alone as the first week at Moravian Seminary for Girls in Green Pond, Pa. I walked around this foreign land, dazed, homesick and disoriented. I called Mother and told her if she didn't come to pick me up I would run away. She very wisely said, "OK. Stay until this weekend and I will come down for a visit. If you still feel the same way, I will bring you home." By the weekend, I wanted no part of going home.

My private moments were spent mourning the loss of Ed. He came once for a visit, rekindling hope, but I did not see him again until my freshman year in college.

My public moments were spent running for class secretary, attending classes, playing field hockey, and learning about other cultures and ethnicities. I spent time internalizing lessons about the importance of self-discipline and deepening my understanding of etiquette, protocols and other nuances so necessary to living a grace-filled life.

Looking back at prep school, I suspect it saved my life. I do believe that without it, I would never have been accepted into college and the course of my life would have taken an entirely different tack. It helped me to understand principles and values that profoundly opened up a much broader world. For the first time in my educational experience, I began to understand the wonder and value of literature and the arts.

I vividly remember how unprepared I felt for the rigorous academic challenges I faced during my first literature class as I tried to make sense of Chaucer's *The Canterbury Tales*. In my public high school a book report retold the story, literally. If your grammar and syntax were correct and you could sufficiently retell the story, you earned an A. Emphasis on themes, symbolism, metaphors and similes was largely absent. My prep school lit class made me feel as if I had wandered into a Latin class! Overwhelmed with a language I did not understand, I was fascinated and terrified all at the same time. I did everything in my power to catch up.

Lillie Turman, headmistress of Moravian Seminary had been engaged to be married, and her fiancé was killed in a jet-fighter accident. As I studied her taut body language and monastic life choices, I suspected she had never recovered from her loss, never married. Lillie Turman's strength of character, her elegance and stoic discipline, her intellect, her devotion to learning and ethical living transformed the way I viewed life. She taught that discipline and protocols matter, and while one has the freedom to break rules, the consequences must be accepted with honor. She barred my roommate and me from attending our senior prom because we had broken school policy by bleaching our hair blonde. I have always been proud that, even though I thought the issue to be absurd, I accepted the consequences honorably.

I was elected by my peers to become Moravian's May Queen. My family attended to see me crowned in the garden behind a fairy tale-like mansion in an "Alice In Wonderland" celebration. As I sat on the dais watching creatures from our "wonderland" perform for my "queenly" pleasure, I found myself thinking about Alice's ability to magically shrink, grow large again, and even change shape. I recognized then that I too, in order to thrive on my ofttimes confusing, sometimes scary, yet magical journey, would need to develop an ability to shrink, grow large and change shape. *How many rabbits might I have to follow into magical holes to grow myself and understand the complexities of my world?* As I sat in the mansion's magnificent formal garden dressed in a gossamer-white gown waiting to have a crown placed on my head, I wondered if there really was such a thing as magic, and if so, could I use that magic to quiet my anguished heart and summon Ed back into my garden.

As my queenly attendant placed the crown upon my head, I wondered if Ed had seen my picture and the announcement in our local newspaper. *Would he simply show up at the celebration?* My eyes continually scanned the crowd in the hope that he would appear. *Maybe magic encounters are only found in fairy tales about girls who follow white rabbits into magic holes, Janet.* He did not come, and he never acknowledged the day. Following the ceremony, as family, friends, and classmates gathered for a luncheon on the patio behind the mansion, I managed to set aside my emotional angst and immersed myself in the excitement and joy of the May Day celebration.

After graduating from prep school and still mourning Ed's loss, I went to Pine Manor Junior College in Wellesley, Massachusetts. I was unaware that Ed knew where I had chosen to go to college, but with his uncanny ability to know where I was at all times, he managed to reappear in my life about every six months.

Sure enough, out of the blue, he called from Brown two weeks before the Christmas break and asked if I needed a ride home. I said yes without a moment's hesitation. My heart leaped with joy, for I had always continued to believe that we would some day be together again. Surely, he would remember and honor all we had been to each other. When he asked me to sit in the middle-front seat next to him on the drive home, I was certain I had been right. The chatter of his four other college friends sharing the ride got lost in my own mental reveries. From time to time his knee would brush mine and my heart would soar. I just knew the Christmas holiday was going to be glorious.

He dropped off all the others, and pulling into our driveway, unloaded my suitcase, wished me a Merry Christmas and drove off. My eyes followed his car until it disappeared. I remained standing in the driveway because I knew I would be able to see his car again as it climbed the steep hill to his house, some quarter-mile away. "He will call, I know he will," I said out loud to myself. I drove past his house almost every day hoping to get a glimpse of him. I suffered through the holiday without hearing from him again.

A college friend drove me back to school after the holidays. I cried myself to sleep every night. My mourning was so intense that one evening I awoke in the middle of the night and felt my father was in the room. His spirit felt so real that I sat up and reached out telling him I knew he was there, that I could feel his presence. I felt he had come to ease my sense of loss, to tell me it was time to accept his death, as well as the end of Ed and my relationship. But I knew in my heart that the loss of my father in combination with the loss of Ed would take many more years to heal.

The summer after my freshman year in college, I decided to take a summer course at Dickinson College in Carlisle, Pa., arranging to carpool with five other students. One of them would become my future husband. Phil was tall, with an athletic build, dark-hair, hazel eyes and a quiet demeanor; I was immediately fascinated. Phil invited me to dinner and a movie as our first carpool trip concluded. We spent every waking summer hour together, swimming, partying, going to the shore, talking about the dreams we might build together. In the fall we both returned to our respective colleges, Phil to Wesleyan, I to Pine Manor. We spent almost every weekend together attending fraternity parties, football games, The Brothers Four and Kingston Trio concerts, or visiting Boston and New York. Mother always teased me that she should have paid my college tuition to Wesleyan rather than Pine Manor.

I graduated from junior college in 1960 and went to work as a private secretary to the credit manager at Harrisburg Hospital. I lived at Mother's farm, but continued to jump on the train most Friday afternoons to spend the weekend at Wesleyan University in Middletown, Connecticut, train back to Harrisburg, jump in my car and drive home to Barleycroft, and then drive back to Harrisburg for work on Monday morning.

An aching stiffness in my neck brought me back to the present on the Cape. I had been sitting on the deck for the entire morning while memories, stored deep inside, emerged. *I need to go for a walk, embrace this beautiful day.* Donning a pair of white shorts, a soft blue chamois shirt, sunglasses and sandals, I slid a few dollars in my pocket and headed up the sandy road to say hi to Joyce and Marty Halpert and talk with them about accepting their earlier dinner invitation.

I spotted Marty working in his garden. A potter friend had given the Halperts a huge green and brown glazed clay pot that Marty had converted into a magnificent fountain. Looking up, he rushed to give me a warm hug and beckoned me to come see the just-completed fountain which had water cascading down over its sides into a bed of smooth black pebbles. A bonsai-shaped pine draped softly over the fountain. He had built a winding steppingstone walk that led from the patio, past the fountain to two beckoning white Adirondack chairs. "Your garden feels as though it is wrapping its arms around me, whispering to me to sit awhile amidst its Zen stillness. Beautiful, absolutely beautiful, Marty."

Joyce had gone to the gym for her thrice-weekly workout, so Marty poured us some iced tea. We settled ourselves into chairs near the hammock to wait for her return. We talked about the intensity of my reflective summer alone, about the loss of Mother and Joan, about life's passages and the healing process that follows sorrow. Marty spoke about some of his own life's passages, and I felt so blessed to be given an opportunity to see more deeply into the soul of this wise and insightful friend.

After a while, when Joyce had not returned, Marty mused that she must have decided to do some errands after her workout. He suggested we do dinner at their house the following evening. I thanked him for the invite and headed down the road to the beach. It was a gloriously sunny day, without a cloud breaking up the intensely blue sky. Neighbors' yards were bursting with pink, blue and white hydrangeas, interspersed with vivid purple Russian sage and yellow Black-Eyed Susans.

My heart was singing inside as I turned toward the bay—
*beautiful friendship, beautiful surroundings . . . so many blessings.
These are the moments we must carefully store in our hearts, so we
can use them to lessen the intensity of the dark times; that's how we
stay strong, how we survive.*

"Listening to silence is hardest of all.
You want to fill it up with conversation.
With noise. With distraction. Resist . . .
In silence you can listen to your own heart-
beat . . . In silence, you can dream great
dreams. You can discover your own music.

Nancy Moon

June Meditation from
DANCING MOONS

CHAPTER FOURTEEN

BARLEYCROFT

U sat on the sand to rest and reflect. As I looked out over the navy-blue sparkling bay, water lapped in hypnotic rhythm against sand and rocks. Peace and stability filled my heart. Memories of Barleycroft, Mother and my stepfather Tom washed over me.

In the summer of 1960, Mother moved Grandfather Clyde, John, Joyce, and me to Barleycroft. My grandfather had owned two farms in York County and leased them to tenant farmers. Over the years, the wear and tear of tenants had taken an enormous toll on the farmhouses, the barns and the surrounding property. My mother, drawing on a dream she and my dad had always had, decided to carry out that dream by restoring one farm to rent, and one for our family to live in. Barleycroft, "fields of barley," was born.

My family's large brick farmhouse was surrounded by 300 acres which were tenant-farmed. Mother completely restored the farm, both inside and out. Her interior design included age-silvered barn siding and deep red-patterned wallpaper on the kitchen walls, gray flag-stone kitchen floors and red tractor seats as bar stools. For parties, two large wood-fired antique copper cauldrons served as soup servers and all five working fireplaces were lit to create a gala atmosphere. Two staircases leading to the second-floor bedrooms, one in the front of the house and the other a steep winding back staircase that led to what previously had been slave quarters, added a touch of historical intrigue. A signed William Penn land-grant document hung over the den's fireplace. A huge Chinese ancestral death scroll, which my father bought for my mother many years previously, hung in the formal Victorian parlor. The foot-deep window sills hinted at sturdy thick brick walls, and when decorated with candles, pinecones, flowers and greens for celebratory occasions, the sills added an additional festive touch.

The physical transformation of the farm was accompanied by a spiritual transformation for our family, providing us with a place of stability and joy, a place where we could all gather. The early years at Barleycroft renewed our sense of family and softened our deep sense of loss precipitated by the death of my father.

Phil and I announced our engagement in December 1961. His grandmother had given Phil a family diamond which we had placed into an antique setting. A few days before our engagement party at Barleycroft, Phil set up a treasure hunt which led me to various sites around the farm. I eventually found my diamond ring inside a snow ball, lying on top of a snow drift, along the road leading to the farm.

Our Christmas holiday engagement party is legend-
ary among attendees. I wore a bold hot pink and gold lamé
dress and gold shoes, which everyone said made me look like
a wrapped Christmas present. Chefs from the local country
club wearing high white hats and starched white jackets served
bubbling soup from the kitchen's copper cauldrons. The dining room table was laden with hors d'oeuvres, baked ham and
turkey with all the trimmings and desserts of every description.
The house glowed with candlelight, three decorated Christmas
trees and fires in all five fireplaces. Greens, bows, and pine cones
decorated every window sill and staircase banister, the bar remained open throughout the night, and the band played in the
kitchen where we and our guests danced on the flagstone floor
until the wee small hours of the morning. I felt exhilarated and
filled with joyful anticipation of our June wedding.

The following morning, Mother enticed Phil's fraternity
brothers out of their sleeping bags by standing in the middle of
the parlor with a pitcher of leftover bourbon-laced Mary Sachs
cocktails asking, "Would anyone care for a drink?" They were
on their feet in a split second, eating eggs, bacon, fish cakes,
fried potatoes and scrapple. After breakfast, Mother brought
the garden hose inside and everyone pitched in with brooms
and mops, washing down the beer-stained flagstone kitchen
floor. Later in the morning, we discovered party revelers sleeping in the hay stacks in the barn. Phil returned to college and I
returned to work a few days after the party.

That spring, my mother called me at work to say that Ed
had called; he had seen the engagement announcement in the
paper and planned to be at the farm when I got home. When I

approached him in the driveway, he blurted out, "Please don't do this. Please don't marry Phil. Can we go somewhere and talk?" I needed time to think. I told him I needed to go in to tell Mother that I was going out.

"Do not go. He will only confuse you" was mother's reply when I told her what Ed had said. I took her advice. When I told Ed that I had decided it would be unwise to go with him, he asked me if I were really sure. I told him I was. As I walked away, my heart felt heavy wondering if it was wise not to hear what he had to say; to seek closure.

The following week, attempting to force final closure, I lit a fire in a large trash barrel and dropped each and every one of Ed's love letters into the flames. Next I threw in an entire scrapbook filled with pictures, old dried corsages, matchbook covers and invitations. I felt as if I were emotionally frozen in time, as the blue and orange flames turned memories into ashes. My burning ceremony did not bring the closure I sought.

Phil graduated from college June 3, 1962, and we were married on June 9. We honeymooned for a week on Nantucket, and upon return, set up our first apartment at Phil's prep school alma mater in Salisbury, Connecticut, amidst the Berkshire Mountains. Phil taught biology, physics, and classical music, and I worked as the school librarian. I loved setting up our apartment, grocery shopping on my own, and exploring our marital relationship, with each of us engaged in meaningful work. It felt so liberating to be on our own. In late spring we learned I was pregnant. I was thrilled, Phil was conflicted.

That summer we drove cross-country to Colorado where Phil took biology courses and I took library science courses, all underwritten by our employer. Every weekend we headed out from our dorm-room to hike the mountains, camp by mountain streams, explore historical sites. We both fell in love with Colorado and pledged to return often. Re-crossing the country at the end of August with little money left, we were forced to sleep in the back of our station wagon and eat sandwiches made with cold meat that floated atop melted ice in our cooler. My large belly made sleeping in the back of the wagon particularly challenging. Our summer was a spectacularly wonderful adventure, a real growing experience for Phil and me.

Back in Connecticut, Mother called to tell me she had just married Tom. Mother, laughing about being dressed in an all black outfit, said she and Tom drove to the justice of the peace, were married, and, an hour later, she was back at her office. Mother had always told us that she would never remarry after Daddy's death, but somewhat apologetically explained that she needed Tom to help her manage the farm.

Years later Mother told me, "He has never touched me, never will." I felt stunned and uncomfortable about Mother feeling the need to declare celibacy since we had never discussed sexuality, not even in my adolescence. I struggled with the morality of Mother's decision to enter a marriage of convenience as a means of staying on the farm. At the time, I considered it a misguided declaration of a decade-long faithfulness to my dad and felt sad for her and Tom, two beautiful adults with so much life to live. On the surface, at least, it appeared to work for both of them. Barleycroft was the bond that held their relationship together—Mother the dreamer and financier, Mother and Tom together, the implementers.

Our daughter Susan was born in Sharon, Connecticut, on December 3, 1963. The following year, Phil took a position at his college alma mater, Wesleyan University in Middletown, Connecticut. Our second daughter Tracy was born November 27, 1964. The births of our two daughters eleven months and three weeks apart startled us significantly. We laughed about our Irish twins and my own mother-elephant-like two year gestation period! My two daughters anointed my life with light; Phil, however, struggled to adapt to being a father and his battle with his inner demons intensified. Angry sporadic uncontrollable outbursts confused both of us and placed strains on our relationship. I sought out the comfort and stability of Barleycroft to assuage my anxieties. The girls and I made the drive to Pennsylvania often, with Phil joining us when his job permitted.

Over many years, Barleycroft continued to evolve and flourish. Laboring together, Mother and Tom built stone walls along the long driveway and a brick wall across the front of the property. Mother contracted to have the barn restored and then leased it to a thoroughbred show-horse trainer. Next to be restored, a spring house with a stream running through the first floor, a large fireplace, bedroom and bath. Mother rented that as well. Together she and Tom oversaw the building of a large spring-fed lake, complete with diving board and sandy beach, and stocked it with carp to control the algae. They bought and restored another property a short distance down the road from the farm, and rented that out, as well. Tom planted peach trees and Mother froze the peaches; they planted a large vegetable garden and Mother canned the abundant harvest. Mother was an excellent cook who could stretch a dollar further than anyone I have ever known. Must have been those German genes, "Waste not, want not."

Whenever the family gathered, it was party time. Mother and Tom often put up a yellow candy-striped tent in the yard to put distance between my grandfather and us—partially because he disapproved of alcohol and parties and partially in deference to his farmer's routine of going to bed at nine o'clock and arising at six.

Party time for the adults meant a basement refrigerator with two spigots on the outside of the door, one with draft beer, one with Coke, and an unlimited supply of wine and liquor, lobsters from Maine, steaks from Omaha, a hot game of volley ball or ping pong, swimming in the lake with tiki torches lighting your way until dawn, breakfasts of bacon, fried potatoes, eggs and scrapple ready when you arose. Whenever I or my siblings visited the farm, we knew that Mother and Tom awakened early, prepared breakfast and loved taking care of any grandchildren who arose early, allowing us the luxury of sleep.

And for the grandchildren, it was taking picnics to the beach by the lake, feeding baby bottles filled with warm milk to newly-born lambs by the kitchen fireplace, riding Spotter the pony, hearing hours of bedtime stories, playing dress-up with old prom gowns from a trunk in the attic, riding on grandmother's or step-grandfather's lap as they drove the small tractor to cut acres of grass, swinging on the striped canvas-roofed tandem swing with Grandmother, Mother, aunts, and as many cousins as we could squeeze on, all the while telling stories of generations past and planning adventures to come. On one occasion, Mother and Tom filled Tom's old red truck with hay from the barn, loaded into the back of the truck their old collie Prince along with all the grandchildren dressed in Halloween costumes, and entered the Mechanicsburg Halloween parade. Mother and Tom loved creating magic for their grandchildren.

Mother eventually decided to retire her stockbroker license, since the numerous rental properties provided all the necessary revenues to keep Barleycroft thriving. Retirement did not deter Mother from continuing to dream as family came and went from the farm. Her final farm project, a couple years before she made the decision to sell the farm, was to reconfigure an old abandoned silo into a round five-story rental home: a glass elevator with a telephone, a view of three counties from the top floor playroom with a built-in bar, lipstick red carpet juxtaposed against stark white walls, a two-story bold red, blue and yellow modernist patterned carpet hanging from the living room wall. Mother had the creative vision, Tom the technical skills. The family had back-to-back parties for a week before renters moved in. The local newspaper interviewed Mother and printed a four-page article with pictures of Barleycroft's unique round silo-house.

As memories of the magnificent three-county-vista from atop the silo faded, and my view returned to the sparkling Cape

Cod Bay, I thought about how magnificently blessed that time had been for all my extended family. It was a sort of respite from the world's travails, our family's magic kingdom.

Rising and brushing the sand from my shorts, I climbed the stairs to the top of the dunes, and headed for the sculpture garden at The Cape Cod Museum of Art. At the main entrance, I noticed that Scargo Pottery's Harry Holl, cofounder of the museum, had donated one of his signature pieces, a fired clay castle that sat on an island in the center of a small pond. I followed the brick walkway towards the entrance. Many bricks had been carved with the names of loved ones, both living and dead, a fundraiser for the museum and a loving tribute to lost loved ones.

Once inside the museum, I realized I was hungry and somewhat fatigued, so I decided to do a cursory walk through the first floor and then purchase a brick to be carved "Victoria and Payton Becker, beloved granddaughters." I giggled thinking about how much fun it would be to bring them to the museum during their visit next summer and see how long it took them to locate their brick. My granddaughters had visited the Cape with their parents every summer. Now they would become a permanent part of Cape Cod. How wonderful, I mused.

I delighted in the museum's current seascape of ships, the sea, and beautiful landscapes. Then I ordered my granddaughter's carved brick and left. Cutting through the museum's parking lot I followed a path through a line of trees to Buckie's Biscotti's, my favorite local pastry shop. There I bought one of their delicious cranberry scones and a Nantucket spice loaf which, when combined with a mellow cup of coffee, would be my week's breakfasts. Finally I headed for home over the inland route, so I could stop at The Marshside for a quick burger and fries. The stars were just beginning to peak out of the sky as I trotted down Tommy's Road for home.

Later crawling into bed, I called Phil and the girls. Everyone assured me that all was well. We wished each other love and sweet dreams.

CHAPTER FIFTEEN

DRAGON'S FIRE

I awoke during the night feeling like my body had been engaged with the forces of darkness. My bedcovers, dampened by sweat, lay crumpled at the foot of my bed. I turned on the light, and glanced at the dreamcatcher to see if it had trapped whatever painful memories had awakened me. As I lay breathing deeply, those memories began to slowly reemerge.

———————✦———————

After my father's death, I had tried to naively console myself by thinking that our family's sacrifices had sufficiently satisfied whatever debt God felt we needed to pay for our sins. Father Simpson, the Catholic priest who presided over our parish, appeared to be more at home with the Old Testament's wrathful God than the forgiving, compassionate New Testament Jesus. Consequently, at twelve years old, devastated by the enormity of the sacrifice, but schooled in Father

Simpson's wrathful, demanding God, I felt afraid to acknowledge my fear and anger with God. I struggled to sublimate Father Simpson's wrathful God, fearing that further sacrifices would be required.

Now, as Phil and I celebrated our two toddler daughters' birthdays amidst balloons, cakes and laughter, I received a phone call from my sister Joan, telling me that my brother and sister-in-law's six-year-old, and only son Johnny, had been run over by a dump truck in front of their home. The words of Father Simpson's wrathful God, "Vengeance is mine," reverberated inside my mind. And the black hole in my heart roiled and deepened.

As I had done during my father's illness, I tried to cut a deal with God. Driving alone through the night from Connecticut to Pennsylvania, I begged and pleaded aloud. "Please, God, let him live and not be permanently damaged. Please, God, don't let this innocent child suffer. Please, God, not their only son."

I drove through the night, my mind consumed with question after question for God. *Why didn't you prevent the dusting of snow, or delay the dump truck by just a moment or two? Why did you allow this small child to borrow someone's snow saucer? Aren't you our all-powerful Father, the perfect parent who would never abandon His child? How in the hell could you have allowed this to happen?* I remember the guilt I felt for being grateful that my children were safe, for being so far away and unable to lend immediate support to my brother and sister-in-law, for cursing God for His indifference, for wondering if God even existed.

Fluctuating between anger towards God and the need to seek his mercy, I struggled to reach out to the New Testament God of love and healing miracles. I begged Him to raise up this child and return him to wholeness and health.

When I crossed into Pennsylvania, I stopped at a gas station and called my sister Joan, who told me that the state police had located my brother John in the mountains where he had gone to hunt and had accompanied him home. Johnny had died. The wrathful God had indeed demanded further sacrifice on our family's stone altar. I hung up the phone, but stood immobilized and in such pain I thought my heart would burst. I cursed God for not showing mercy by calling out at the last moment, as he had done to spare Abraham's son Isaac. "You could have called it off," I cried. "You could have called it off. This small child was one of your most beautiful and innocent angels. Why, damn it, why?"

I stumbled to the car. Sadness for my sister-in-law and brother overwhelmed me to the point of numbness. I struggled with how best to help them through their excruciatingly painful journey. I sobbed for them, knowing that nothing would ever lift this burden from their hearts, nor from the hearts of all who knew and loved this special child.

After arriving at my brother's house, I was asked to call Good Shepherd Catholic Church to request priestly guidance and support. As the phone rang, I thought about how years ago my birth family had left this church following my dad's death due to its insensitivity and inappropriate responses to our family's loss. Our family had long since stopped attending Good Shepherd Church. Ironically, many years later, my sister-in-law had chosen Catholicism and Good Shepherd parish as her spiritual home.

When I explained what had happened, the nun who had answered the phone asked, "Are they members in good standing?" I was stunned into silence. She put down the phone, and I heard the rustling of papers. I realized she was checking her files to see if my brother and sister-in-law had tithed adequate dollars to warrant the church responding. When the nun got back on the phone, I made it very clear how cruel I considered her response and hung up. The church did send a priest later in the day to talk with my brother and sister-in-law about their loss and to make funeral arrangements.

My family buried that beautiful little blonde-haired boy with his stuffed duck in a tiny casket beside my father of the same name. The duck Johnny called Ronald McDonald had belonged to my daughters but they had given it to him because he loved it so. It warmed my heart to know he was not alone, that a small part of his cousins' love was with him. Another part of each of us died on that cold desolate winter day.

⸺⸺⸺⬦⸺⸺⸺

Back in Connecticut, reflecting on Johnny's death, I began to suspect that if there was a God, He did not intervene on earth. How else could I reconcile a compassionate God with Johnny's death? What a terrifying notion, I thought. *If God does not intervene on earth, then there is no one to curse in the darkness and no one to thank in the light.*

Feeling exhausted and overwhelmed by the memories of Johnny's death, I willed myself back to sleep. I re-awakened a few hours later.

"No matter how hard the loss,
defeat might serve as well
as victory to shape
the soul and let the glory out."

Vice-President Al Gore

CHAPTER SIXTEEN

MARITAL BOOKENDS

*F*eeling emotionally restless, I reached for the book on my bedside table that a friend had recently recommended: Joan Anderson's, *A Year By The Sea*. Anderson spent a year alone on the Cape, seeking herself and gaining perspective on her marital challenges. The similarities of our journey astounded me.

As I read, I felt that Anderson must have lived for a time inside my soul, for she seemed to know my secrets. She too had married a melancholy man who had had a difficult childhood. She too was the ultimate caregiver who had been "challenged by his shadows." Anderson thought she'd "fix his melancholia somehow, lifting him above the darkness he had grown so used to carrying." I had naively thought the same. She too ultimately found herself "feeling more and more oppressed by a role she had undoubtedly created." She loved, as I loved, by "giving and giving until I saw the pleasure of my efforts on the other's face." Anderson's marital walk was so similar to my own that her words left me breathless.

Her husband thought of his "primary role as breadwinner." She "filled weekends with people and parties, hoping to ignite his spirit, but often such occasions made him retreat all the more." As I read Anderson's reflections, I thought about my own efforts to "ignite Phil's spirit." Phil's administrative responsibilities included attending and holding frequent social events. At the time, I felt angry and confused not realizing that Phil felt safe in public spaces, challenged and unsafe in private family spaces. Not fully understanding that his spirit had been extensively pummeled by a childhood environment that lacked the love and support so essential to growing a child's resilient heart, confusion and angst filled my heart. Uncontrollable "fight or flight" anxiety filled our home with anticipatory angst; always waiting for the next disheartening confrontation. Some would call it "walking on eggshells." Anderson's book had unearthed extremely uncomfortable memories that had been lurking beneath my consciousness. Feelings of anxiousness, sadness, guilt and apprehension rose up from deep within.

I reassured myself by remembering that an examination of Mother's and my relationship had shaken loose the same guilty feelings. But by persevering, I had discovered such examinations ultimately produce insights and understanding, strengthening rather than diminishing love. Now, I must tamp down my feelings of spousal disloyalty in order to fully examine Phil's and my relationship. Anderson's book provided guideposts and insights to light my way. I could not put the book down until I had completed it. As I read the last page, the first light of dawn began to appear in the sky.

I was emotionally exhausted and fell back to sleep. I awakened to discover the hands of the alarm clock pointing to twelve noon. *Truly, I am resonating to my own rhythms, making my own time. What a marvelous luxury.*

As I dressed leisurely, I felt passages from Anderson's book shaking loose memories that I knew I needed to acknowledge. Downstairs, I poured myself a glass of iced tea, grabbed a cranberry scone, and went to the deck to review the passages that had spoken to my heart, passages that I wanted to note in my journal.

Enjoying my lunch in the gloriously sunlit afternoon, I heard a soft buzzing by my ear; my little hummingbird friend had reappeared. "You know, don't you?" I whispered. "You know what an arduously long journey I made during the night and how discouraged I feel about having the tenacity to complete the journey, don't you? You have come to remind me that your tiny wings, beating with determination and grit, sustain you in your yearly 2,500 mile challenging journey to and from South America. You put me to shame, tiny one."

As he flew sideways out of sight, I thought I could hear him say, *"Janet, if I can do it, you can do it too. With determination and grit, seemingly overwhelmingly impossible journeys become possible."* His wise counsel summed up my summer odyssey and described the bookends of my marriage: overwhelmingly impossible at one end, determination and grit stacked in the middle, and nothing being impossible at the other end.

The earliest years of my marriage represented the over-whelmingly impossible bookend. I brought to my marriage a driving need for control, certainty and safety. Phil brought melancholia and emotional outbursts that threatened to over-whelm our marriage and served to exacerbate my driving life-long needs for safety, security and unconditional love. Our marital dysfunction tore at my heart.

Compounding our inability to effectively communicate with one another, Phil's college administrative career placed enor-mous demands on both of us. Entertaining trustees, attending most college functions, being supportive friends to the college president and his wife all added further pressure as I struggled to reconcile my confused and brokenhearted private emotions with the need to publicly perform. We both became so skilled at public performances that even the college president and his wife, dear friends with whom we spent enormous amounts of time, did not suspect any marital difficulties. My accumulating emotional scars left me feeling alone, angry and alienated, and left our children to absorb our home's anxious sadness.

The death of my nephew, Johnny, re-enforced my un-derstanding that life can and does steal loved ones in an in-stant. In reaction, I fearfully hovered over our daughters. Phil, who had never experienced appropriate nurturing, struggled to parent himself and was unable to parent our daughters. Be-lieving that if I loved them enough so that the girls would be protected from any negative fallout, I became a single parent, determinedly focused on their well-being. I believed that if I vigilantly circled them with love, I could minimize any perma-nent damage being done to their spirits.

I found protective solace within family. Phil found protective solace in dark places and whenever life's difficulties threatened to overwhelm him, he would quickly retreat into his carefully constructed dark cave and roll the stone in front of the entrance. I was left alone. It took me many years to learn that it was unwise to stand at the mouth of the cave asking if I had done something wrong, urgently calling to him to come out so we could figure out the darkness together. It only forced him to retreat even more deeply. I grew to understand that my only recourse was to go on with my life, as best I could, and wait for him to re-emerge. A sense of aloneness and sadness threatened to overwhelm me.

Looking back, I suspect that coaching men's and women's rowing teams on the beautiful Connecticut River provided another form of retreat, allowing Phil to spend countless hours immersed in a world of water, boats and physical prowess. He took great pride in shaping both the bodies and minds of young college men and women and left me the exclusive responsibility of shaping our daughters' lives. A part of me felt proud of Phil's coaching achievements, but in the deepest recesses of my heart I struggled to control the resentment I felt about the sacrifices required of both me and my daughters.

At the same time, I began to worry that his focused attention to his volunteer crew activities was undermining his administrative effectiveness. I tried to point out to Phil that his concentrated efforts as crew coach might be jeopardizing his job. "That's ridiculous. It may be voluntary, but crew is part of my job," he responded. Finally, the president, our close friend, approached me to ask if I could refocus Phil's energies back to his primary responsibilities. I told him that I had been sensing his frustration, had spoken to Phil on numerous occasions, but had failed to convince him of the merits of my observations. I suggested that he might be able to succeed where I had failed. He indicated he had been unsuccessful as well.

Phil's and my inability to communicate created a marital vacuum, a dangerous emotional disconnect. Each time I tried to reach out to him, he retreated ever more deeply into his dark psychological cave, rolling a boulder of denial in front of the opening to ensure no one could enter.

Then one day my spirit collapsed into a deep depression. I was unable to function. Seated on a couch in our family room, I began to cry uncontrollably and simply could not make myself get up. I sat mired in a sort of gauzy limbo, unable to speak, unable to control my tears, unwilling to continue to try. Phil attempted to talk with me. My inability to rise up out of my spiritual exhaustion frightened both Phil and me.

Deeply concerned, Phil called Mother in Pennsylvania and asked if she would come to Connecticut to help us sort through our difficulties. The three of us spent the weekend talking about complicated emotions and identifying possible next steps. As we spoke, I realized that I wished to leave Connecticut and return to live in Pennsylvania, with or without Phil. After Mother left, I shared that desire with Phil, and his immediate response was that he would accompany me home.

After making the decision to move, Phil returned to the office. At first, I found myself sitting in exhausted silence. Then, suddenly, I began rushing jubilantly around the house, screaming at the top of my lungs with tears of joy cascading down my cheeks, "I'm going home. I'm going home. Thank God, I'm going home." Going "home" meant I would have a loving and supportive platform from which I might right myself and possibly my marriage. It also meant I would never be unavailable to my birth family should tragedy strike again. Even in the midst of my emotional chaos, I felt a glimmer of affection for this man who had chosen to follow me home.

We talked that evening about what he might do. When he responded that he had always had white-collar jobs and would welcome an opportunity to get his hands dirty, I mentioned that my brother John was thinking about starting his own construction company and that they should talk when we were at Barleycroft for Thanksgiving.

Over the holiday, after speaking with my brother, Phil decided to leave college administration after ten years and join him in forming a utility construction company. We traveled back to Connecticut, Phil gave notice of his departure, and we said our good-byes to startled friends.

As my thoughts shifted back to the moment and my beloved Cape, I realized I was due at the Halperts' for dinner in a half hour. Snuggling down among good friends seemed like a perfect ending to the twenty-four hours through which I had just struggled. I pulled on a clean pair of shorts and shirt, selected a gift bottle of wine from the bar, and walked up the sandy road. Marty and Joyce's house is filled with art work collected during their travels. Glowing heart-pine floors adorned with oriental carpets, an extensive collection of handmade ceramics, and eclectically interesting furniture all contribute to a feeling of warmth and graciousness. Thoughtfully generous, they oversee our Cape house when we are not there, and often tend to our spirits as well. Phil and I have often spoken of how blessed we feel to have them as our friends.

When I arrived, Marty was making one of his delicious tossed salads. Joyce was busily finishing up the last few touches on the dinner table. Marty poured us each a drink and we retired to their backyard to immerse ourselves in their miniature Zen garden. My heart felt nurtured and at peace. We caught up on the comings and goings of our kids, talked about a trip to China that Marty and Joyce were planning. I filled them in on Phil's plans to spend the last week of the summer on the Cape and I brought them up to date on how my summer ruminating was progressing.

We had a delicious candlelight dinner, sharing laughter about all the good times we have had together over many summers. After dinner, after thanks, hugs, and promises to stay in touch, I said my good-byes.

As I walked down the pitch black road, with the bog toads peeping softly, I wondered how many places are left on earth where you can walk in total darkness. Most of the houses that surround our Cape house are only occupied intermittently, so we often have the lovely experience of total darkness. I have treasured the darkness and the night sky for over thirty years.

As I climbed into bed, thinking about yet another evening with close friends, I prayed that the blessings of good friends and this beautiful place would continue to heal my blistered soul.

CHAPTER SEVENTEEN

WOUNDED SPACES COLLIDING

As I awakened the following morning, the sun was shining through my bedroom window, creating fireworklike reflections on the bedroom walls. I knew it was going to be a beautiful day! I promised myself that I would walk to the harbor restaurant for breakfast before I began to read.

Rather than my normal route to the harbor past the sheep farm, I took the left fork the road which passes one lovely home after another. In particular, "the Stone mansion," a turn-of-the-century rambling Cape Cod home situated on ten acres of land with an unimpeded one-hundred-and-eighty degree view of Cape Cod Bay, always gave me pause to dream about life lived in such a gracious home.

Arriving at the harbor restaurant with threateningly gray clouds beginning to gather in the blue sky, I ate my egg and cheese sandwich and iced coffee with haste and headed home.

Settling on the couch with my journal, I reviewed a few sketchy notations I had previously made about both good times and bad which Phil and I experienced after our move from Connecticut to Pennsylvania.

* ———————— >✕< ————————— *

Additional memories emerged: our small house on 24th Street, six blocks from where I had grown up; my work with a real estate firm; Susan and Tracy's entrance into third grade; and Phil and my brother John's establishment of a construction company. Feeling emotionally less vulnerable with the nearness to my birth family from which I had always drawn strength, as well as excited about the formation of the new construction company, I felt cautiously optimistic that our marital difficulties could be overcome. The fight-or-flight instincts I had experienced in Connecticut diminished, but re-emerged a few months later.

I had naively hoped that the move back to Pennsylvania would magically resolve our marital conflicts, but the tensions continued to escalate. Sitting in my real estate office, my heart throbbing with hopelessness and despair, I decided to pick up the girls after school, leave a note for Phil, and move to Barleycroft. I jumped up from my chair, drove home, threw armloads of clothes and our basset hound in the car, picked up the girls at school and drove to Mother's farm. The decision to leave Phil left my heart in excruciating anguish. Leave him? Stay with him? I felt overwhelmed with grief for myself, for my daughters, and for Phil.

Mother, Tom and I talked for hours about my marital difficulties, about miscommunications, incompatibilities, and insensitivities, about the emotional exhaustion I felt attempting to please Phil and keep his melancholia at bay. When Phil got home from work and found my note, he called the farm and spoke to Mother, expressing his disbelief that we had problems severe enough to warrant such a move on my part. He expressed his love for me and our daughters. Together "they" agreed that he and I should sit down and talk. He told Mother that he would come immediately. Mother informed me that Phil was on his way to speak with me and I was furious with her. "I'm not going to see him!" I shouted. "If I see him I will weaken, and I don't want to weaken."

"Janet, you need to speak to your husband and try to work things out, for you as well as the girls."

"Well, I'm not sure I will come downstairs when he arrives. I don't want to see him, maybe the girls and I would be better off without him in our lives. I'm sick of fulfilling the classic women's role of cajoling with smiles and niceties, pretending to the outside world all is well," I sulkily asserted. "I'm going to work on developing a warrior-woman's armor like you, Mother. Be less solicitous and compliant, become more self-protectively assertive."

"There are costs associated with being a warrior woman. Be careful what you wish for," Mother replied. "It's best to find some sort of balance between classically compliant and warrior. I'm going downstairs now. I will let you know when Phil arrives."

I sat on a chair in my old bedroom looking out over the undulating farmland thinking about Phil. He had not had a magical kingdom during his childhood. His mother and father divorced when he was five. His mother remarried a possessive and emotionally challenged man, who drank heavily and eventually became an alcoholic. His stepfather had an erratic temper, a need for control and a jealous nature that extended to his own son as well as his stepson. His mother, fearing another unsuccessful marriage, lacked the will to intervene on Phil and his half-brother's behalf. She made it clear that she never really wanted any children.

As a consequence, Phil carried within himself many torn and bruised spaces, wounds that required all his strength to emotionally sustain himself. From time to time, his emotional vulnerabilities erupted. In Connecticut, I had convinced myself that if I ran hard enough, fast enough, was perfect enough, pleasing enough, I could heal Phil's wounded spaces, stabilize our marriage, and shelter our two daughters from any permanent negative fallout.

Over the years, my wounded spaces have often collided with Phil's, creating angst, confusion and sorrow. My priorities have always been family, since family represented my source of strength and safety, a bulwark against life's difficulties. My background drove deep within my being that family takes priority over all other facets of one's life. Phil's priorities have always been public, because family always represented painful, dysfunctional space, and public activities provided him with his sense of safety. Our public versus private priorities clashed often whether we were discussing donating money to charity or to our children, focusing on the well-being of our daughters or on the well-being of institutions and organizations.

However, each time we have reached what feels like an insurmountable impasse and teeter on the edge of a marital precipice, we have managed to reach out to one another. *Phil is reaching out to you now, Janet. Try to find enough forgiveness in your heart to reach out to him as well. There is so much riding on your decision.*

Maybe our ability to avoid marital disaster stems from the traumas of our previous lives, when Phil lost his father through divorce, and I lost my father through death. I suspect that the anguish of those early traumas established an instinctive willingness to do whatever was necessary to avoid experiencing another utterly life-shattering loss. Remember what it feels like to lose someone you love. Love requires many sacrifices; you know that, Janet, I whispered to myself. And besides, your lifelong need to save suffering rabbits makes it damn unlikely you will be able to turn your back on this man, so get real.

I heard Mother call from the bottom of the stairs telling me Phil had arrived. I knew as I descended the stairs that I loved him and would return home. I also knew that he and I had to find more meaningful ways to communicate. We talked together for some time. In the end, we promised each other that we would both work harder to communicate our grievances and actively address each other's needs. The girls and I returned home with Phil.

My mind cautioned me to remain emotionally vigilant. Even as Phil's and my relationship stabilized, my heart argued otherwise. *Go ahead, my heart shouted, there's no need to be emotionally vigilant. Your marriage and life has stabilized. All is well. Relax, enjoy, and embrace life fully.*

I renewed old friendships and immersed myself again in Barleycroft and family gatherings. I became involved with volunteer work, family activities and successfully ran for Camp Hill Borough Council, the same council my dad had been elected to many years before in spite of his declining health. He had been sworn on to council just a few months before he died.

Twenty-two years later, I was sworn to serve the same community and seated in his chair. I remember saying inside my head to my dad, *"They tell me as long as I'm alive you will never be dead because we look so much alike. That brings me no comfort, for you are gone and I miss you terribly. I am proud to serve what I consider your term, Dad. I will work hard to make you proud. Thank you for being my dad."*

Realizing that marital and family rumination had consumed my afternoon, I drove to Captain Frosty's, a local seafood shack, for a lobster roll and a chocolate frappe. As I sat on the patio eating my dinner, I thought about Victoria and Payton who exclaimed often that Captain Frosty's was their favorite restaurant on the Cape. I wondered how they were doing and decided to call Tracy when I got home.

Back at the house, I made a quick call to Tracy and spoke with both of the girls. They giggled when I told them I had gone to Captain Frosty's and thought of them with love. Knowing all was well at Tracy's, I made a quick call to Susan and she, too, reassured me that all was well with her. One more call, I thought, before I collapse into bed. I talked with Phil for some time, catching up on news from home and filling him in on my Cape Cod wanderings.

Climbing into bed, I reflected on the day's insights: marital difficulties driven by parallel perceptions of safe spaces, of public versus private loyalties; the tenacity of the human spirit to not only endure losses but to learn from them. As I rolled over to squeeze Payton's dreamcatcher, I wondered what other challenging insights would be caught in its web in the morning light.

"Out of every crisis,
comes the chance to be reborn."

Nena O'Neill

CHAPTER EIGHTEEN

UPHEAVALS

I awakened in the morning to see raindrops sliding like silver-mercurial beads down the windows and splattering onto the deck below. Dark thunderous clouds hung suspended over the bay's roiling waters, warning of turbulent moments ahead. I could not see Provincetown, and the water had disappeared into the gossamer-like gray fog hanging over the cranberry bog. The end of the backyard looked like it was the end of the earth. I love all the moods of the Cape. Summer thunderstorms accompanied by fog make me feel enclosed and safe in a caterpillar-like metamorphic cocoon. *Sacred times to grow my soul until my wings are strong enough to fly.*

I grabbed my bathrobe, ran downstairs to fix myself a quick bagel and coffee, then returned upstairs to settle myself into an easy chair facing the raging turbulence. As I sat watching the rain, I spotted a book lying on the table next to my chair. Just reading the title, *New Hope for Binge Eaters*, brought horrendously difficult memories surging into my mind, and my thoughts returned to Susan's struggle to cast out demons.

Tracy, age fourteen, found a young man to whom she could open her heart, and so began to spend less time with family. Her peer group expanded and she began to fly. Susan did not find a special other, had limited peer contact, and as a result began to turn inward. Socially engaged and yet having developed a quiet sensitivity to her sister's struggle, Tracy found herself caught in a tension-filled dilemma.

I rushed to fill the void created by my daughters' differing circumstances, hoping to free Tracy to fully fly and to limit Susan's comparative angst. Susan and I began to spend a lot of time together cooking, shopping, and generally enjoying each other's companionship. But I sensed a quiet change in her that I could not put into words.

I began to lie awake at night worrying about the cause; missing Tracy's companionship was a possibility, but the melancholia I saw overshadowing Susan's loving personality appeared far more deep-seeded. I questioned myself. Had I made a mistake staying in a conflicted marriage that produced anxiousness in our home? Or would martial commitment in the face of conflict ultimately prove helpful in our daughters' future marriages? Was Susan experimenting with drugs? The only agonizing option open to me was to remain supportive, wait and carefully watch for clues that might identify the source of my daughter's difficulties.

My struggle to understand Susan was a backdrop to other major life-altering shifts. With the death of my Grandfather Clyde, in combination with less frequent visits by me and my siblings, Barleycroft became more difficult for Mother to sustain, both emotionally and financially. In 1977, she sold the farm, telling each of her children to select a few items they particularly loved before the country auction. Another traumatic loss for our entire family, but Mother again led the way, never faltering, never showing emotion, just realistically understanding that the sale was simply something that had to be done. My stepfather, Tommy, fought the decision, but as always Mother prevailed. Mother carried Barleycroft in her heart until she died, often parking her car nearby the farmhouse to reflect and reminisce.

Mother always knew that when it came time to sell Barleycroft, she would return to Camp Hill where she and my dad had spent their happiest years. I accompanied Mother and a realtor friend as we looked at numerous houses, including a home just a couple of doors down from where Phil, the girls and I lived. Mother did not think the house would meet her and Tom's needs, but I thought it might meet ours. Mother proposed that she buy our house and Phil and I buy the larger house. Phil agreed. Mother moved into our home, we moved two doors and a dog's leg down the street.

Throughout Mother's and our resettlement, Susan's struggles and my concerns continued to deepen. One afternoon I went into my daughter's bathroom and picked up a book that was opened and upside down on the back of the toilet. Glancing at the title, *New Hope For Binge Eaters*, the words binge eaters puzzled me. What is binge eating? I asked myself. As I read the first couple pages, I began to sob. "Oh, dear Lord," I shouted, "this is what's been happening to Susan." Clutching the book to my chest, I ran down the hall to Susan's bedroom, sat down on her bed, pulled back the covers under which she hid herself most days after school, and said, "Susan, this is you, isn't it, sweetheart?"

"Yes," she cried.

Pope and Hudson's book is an expose of the eating disorder demon, bulimia. A compulsive eating-purging-depressive disorder, bulimia drives its victims to secretly and compulsively consume enormous amounts of food, then purge with laxatives or forced throwing up to eliminate weight gain. Feelings of depression, anxiety, guilt and hopelessness follow, sometimes leading to suicide. The book emphasized that like other compulsive addictions, once a bulimic, always a bulimic. It stressed that professional therapy was essential to controlling the disorder.

Susan had begun gaining weight when she was a sophomore in high school and had initiated the bulimic ritual as a means of weight control, as well as to satisfy an emotional need to punish herself for her perceived imperfections. She had discovered *New Hope For Binge Eaters* on the library's shelf a short while before she was scheduled to leave for college. My instincts told me that Susan would be emotionally and physically unable to handle college, but Susan felt she wanted to try it. She began therapy with a children's behavioral therapist recommended by a friend. It didn't help. Between Susan's inability or unwillingness to provide insights into her emotional struggles and the inadequate skills of the therapist, little if any progress was made. Susan went off to her father's alma mater, Wesleyan University, desperately struggling to overcome her compulsions. When she lost all control over her addiction, she sought help from the college psychiatrist and called me every-day, emotionally distraught.

I knew Susan would not survive if I did not bring her home for concentrated professional help. Phil felt she should stay at college and work it out through the college psychiatric counseling services. I agonized. During his Sunday sermon, our pastor-friend must have seen something in my face that concerned him, for he arrived at our backdoor following the church service.

"What in the world is going on, Janet?" he asked. I told him I needed to bring Susan home or she would implode, and I explained why but was agonizing about how to convince Phil.

"Based on what you have told me, I think you should go as soon as you can. Would you like me to join you as you discuss this with Phil? I might be able to be helpful."

As the three of us talked, it became clear that my instincts to bring Susan home were the correct course of action. I called Susan and told her to pack her bags because her father and I would be arriving the next day to bring her home.

Once on campus, we dropped by the infirmary to meet with Susan's doctor. He told us he was relieved and very grate-ful that we had come to take Susan home. He elaborated on Susan's physical and emotional challenges, which he described as severe and recommended a medical leave of absence. We thanked him for all he had done for Susan and told him we would be in touch should she decide to return to Wesleyan.

When Susan opened her dorm room door, my fears were more than confirmed. Dressed in a gauzy Indian-style dress, her weight loss was apparent. The doctor had told us that Susan had been attempting to control her weight issues by starving herself and that the extremely restrictive diet was damaging her kidneys. Appearing weak and pale, it was evident that Susan had physically and emotionally exhausted her body's resources. She fell into my arms.

When we arrived back in Pennsylvania, I suggested that Susan go to her bedroom and not come out until she felt ready to do so. "I will put your meals outside your door. Rest a while, sweetheart, just rest." The next day I was on my knees working in the garden when the back door opened and Susan settled herself in a lawn chair turning her face towards the sun. I continued to garden, barely breathing.

"Mom," she said, "you know you saved my life, don't you?"

I thought I would choke to death trying to suppress my urge to wail. "Yes, sweetheart, I know."

"You are a wonderful Mother. You have always been my light. I will always be grateful to you. Thank you. Do you realize how many of my peers I left behind who will die because their parents are more interested in saving face or simply are too busy with their own lives to take the time to save them?"

"I'm so sorry, Susan. How tragic. All we can hope for is that they, or their parents, will find the courage to seek the help they need. When you are ready, Susan, we will sit down with Dad and figure out the next steps. There is no hurry, take as much time as you need."

Over the next few weeks, Susan slowly began to regain her emotional balance, and we began to search for a therapist who might help her to more fully understand her struggle. We found a therapist in Philadelphia, and Susan began what turned out to be a therapeutic journey for our entire family. I felt some semblance of relief knowing we were beginning to get appropriate professional help.

Almost immediately another challenge arose.

For nine years Brady Contracting had thrived. I worked as office manager for four years, cherishing every day that I could be part of Phil's and my brother John's professional and personal lives. But gradually things began to deteriorate. It appeared as a quiet tension hanging in the air, words unspoken while body language and temperaments silently shouted, "Trouble ahead!" At first, I thought I might be a positive go-between, a bridge between antagonists. But tensions continued to escalate as a passive-aggressive war played itself out. During the last year-and-a-half, all three of our bodies and minds were practically torn apart.

That emotional pressure felt like I was drowning. "For better or worse, in sickness and in health, until death do us part" ran through my mind over and over again. I loved my husband and loved working by his side. Working with my brother every day reconnected me with all my fond memories of times spent playing side-by-side when we were young. Now these idyllic circumstances were disintegrating before my eyes, and I had no ability to change the outcome. Management issues had led to confrontation between two extremely different personalities.

Every day the tensions increased. Every day I prayed John and Phil would reconcile their differences so my heart could remain in tact. That was not to be. I can still hear my brother saying to me, "No matter how this all works out, I want you to know I love you."

I assured him I knew that and that I loved him too, no matter what. "You need to do what you need to do. In time, it will be OK." It was decided that my brother, as majority share holder, would buy out Phil's shares in the company.

Phil decided to return to college administration. This meant our family moving, my giving up the borough council seat, and saying goodbye to many friends. It also meant relinquishing any hope of being the heir apparent as the next state representative. Most importantly, it meant giving up working for the two men I loved most in the world.

The weight of life's burdens pressing on my soul made it increasingly difficult to breathe. My marriage and my emotional stability were threatened by the business decisions being made, decisions over which I had no control. Susan did not seem to be making any strides toward taking hold of her anguished issues. I was standing in a field full of rabbits that were frantically rushing here and there looking for a safe place to hide. I would have to choose which rabbits I would try to save. I could not save them all. I was suffocating emotionally.

Mother, the person I usually turned to for solace and advice, compounded my anguish by siding with my brother. He was all right; Phil was all wrong. Mother had always strongly supported John and John relied on Mother for her counsel. I suspected he must have shared his perspective on office tensions with her, even though the mutual decision had been made to not involve her in office politics. From Mother's comments, I knew Mother had become involved, involved in a way that I felt was unbalanced. I attempted to explain office tensions from my perspective to re-balance a very precarious familial situation. As my anger and confusion increased about the imbalance in all my discussions with Mother, I became increasingly adamant that she didn't know all the facts so she should remain out of the fray. Of course, she did not. Tensions in our relationship escalated. I kept telling myself that the company breakup and potential move away from my hometown were just another loss that I would have to absorb. I felt like I was hanging on by my fingernails. *I cannot do this. I cannot choose. Maybe, somehow, I can save all the rabbits,* I fantasized.

When Mother called and said she would like me to stop by, I heard an angry alienation in her voice. Emotionally fragile and extremely nervous, I walked up to her house. She was waiting for me on the screened porch when I arrived, her face and body language menacingly rigid.

"Sit down, Janet, I need to talk to you," she said icily. My body tensed and my heart beat wildly, emotionally reverting to a childhood response of maternal disapproval. Feeling my legs begin to quiver, I lowered myself into a chair. "I have decided to withdraw my power of attorney, which as you recall, I have given to you and John. I do not feel that you have the best interests of this family at heart, and therefore I have decided withdrawal of your power is the best course of action."

I felt as if she had slapped me across the face, and felt tears tearing at my heart, leaving me breathless. I was heartbroken. I was being punished for trying to support my husband, as well as my brother, through a horrific transition. I had become her enemy for aggressively reminding Mother that there are always two sides to every situation and how important it was to try to balance our perspectives under these family circumstances. Mother saw my anger and frustration as disloyal acts against my birth family. Her power-of-attorney move was a desperate act to force my hand: birth family or husband.

Devastated, and attempting to hold onto some semblance of prideful control, I did not argue with her decision to withdraw the power of attorney. I simply replied, "It is your decision to make, Mother." I immediately rose and left her house.

As I walked home with tears streaming down my face, I thought, all right, Mother, you have tried to use guilt and manipulation to control what I do. I found myself asking a painful question. *Is it possible that my mother, who had always professed unconditional and exceptional love for her children, would destroy me to win?* My aching heart told me that our mother-daughter relationship had forever been transformed. I felt abandoned and trapped in an emotional morass that had painful consequences no matter where I turned.

———◆✕◆———

I stopped in the park across from our house, sat down in the grass and searched my memory for answers to why Mother had chosen to compound my anguish at such a vulnerable time. Why? During my childhood, she had often said, "Remember where you come from; family loyalty should be a top priority." More accurately, she should have said birth-family loyalty is everything, because she tolerated, but never really supported any in-laws. She often ferried hurtful stories, shared confidences between siblings and those they'd married. This put a tremendous stress on all her children's marriages. Mother, as the matriarchal center, undermined meaningful adult relationships between siblings by keeping them suspiciously isolated from each other. Mother managed to make sure that almost all communication between siblings went through her, while at the same time insisting that love and loyalty between siblings was paramount. Now, her aggressive actions held the potential to drive a wedge between my brother and me, as well as to undermine my marriage.

By the time I arose I said to myself, *"Janet, you have done nothing wrong. You are desperately trying to resolve this heart-breaking loss without disloyalty to anyone."* I thought again about John and my exchange as we both confronted the necessity to divide the company. "No matter what happens," John had said as his voice broke, "I want you to remember I love you. Always have, always will."

Choking on emotional anguish, I had replied, "And I will love you always as well, no matter what. There is no turning back now. In time, it will be OK."

I repeated those words out loud to myself as I walked home from the park, realizing that there had been no disloyalty; it was an exchange of love between a brother and a sister, a recognition that under such circumstances the best expression of love for each other was to hug and walk away.

I sat down in our garden to think further about the power-of-attorney incident. By withdrawing her power of attorney, in the words of that document, she was "serving notice to the world [that I no longer] had the power to act on behalf of my mother." In my mother's eyes, I was no longer trustworthy, no longer loyal enough to my birth family to handle her affairs. She needed to punish me.

Withdrawing the power of attorney was designed to deliver a severe blow in a battle to intimidate and weaken the resolve of her foe. Life had always taught my mother that she had to be a warrior. Effective warriors always plan to win, fight to the death, if necessary. My mother's warrior power, when juxtaposed against my instinctual need to save all rabbits left me at a distinct disadvantage whenever we did battle.

As it turns out, it was an emotionally damaging, but ultimately hollow act of war. Because when she entered a retirement home and became unable to handle her affairs, I would visit each week to pay her bills, bring her books on tape, and take her out to dinner. I always included her in activities in both our home in Lancaster as well as at our vacation homes. During her last few years of life, she would often say, "What would I ever do without you and Joyce? I would be lost and alone." Mother and I never discussed the power of attorney issue again.

In time, I came to understand her threat to withdraw her power of attorney was merely a tactical battle strategy to persuade me to choose my brother's side in the company break up and remain living in Camp Hill, a couple doors down from Mother. I have no evidence that Mother ever changed her power of attorney. In time, the welts on my heart finally healed, and I came to understand that Mother's gesture was the angry response of a mother who felt she was losing her daughter not only from down the street, but quite possibly her daughter's heart. The pain and loneliness of those thoughts, deep within my mother's soul, caused her instinctively to choose her own well-being over that of her daughter. At work were innate instincts bred into her throughout her lonely childhood.

Phil returned to college administration, making the round-trip two-hour commute to Lancaster's Franklin and Marshall College for about a year. For practical reasons, it became necessary to move, and many friendships and opportunities died in the ashes of our departure from Camp Hill. Shortly before the move, Susan's therapeutic struggles were compounded by her therapist's move out of state. We could hardly believe that three years of therapeutic investment had been wiped out in an instant. We began the arduous task of finding a replacement in the midst of our move to Lancaster.

As the thunderstorms over Cape Cod Bay abated, I grabbed my journal determined to document painful emotional transitions and lessons learned. *Writing is such a powerful exorcism. Maybe if I commit thoughts to paper, maybe they will be exorcised from my heart.* As I wrote, I realized that the move to Lancaster had freed me from the daily influence of my mother, allowed me to begin to hear my own voice and ultimately created the circumstances that allowed me to graduate from Franklin and Marshall College, run for local political office and work for Pennsylvania's Governor.

Truly, life has a way of leading us where we need to go.

CHAPTER NINETEEN

WARRIOR'S ARMOR

Writing about my challenging memories had consumed the rainy morning. With half the day gone, I was determined to get out into the sunshine. As the rays of light peeked through the rain clouds, I packed a light lunch, checked the tide clock to make sure the tide was low, donned my swimsuit, slathered myself with lotion, grabbed a towel and a beach chair, and walked the short distance to the beach. At low tide a three-hundred-foot sandy beach stretches to the water's edge, with another two-hundred-foot stretch of soft white sand underfoot in waste-deep clear blue water.

I dropped my things on the sand, and dashed for the water. Floating aimlessly with the arms of the sea wrapped around me, my thoughts returned to my family's therapeutic efforts to right itself.

Our third therapist, Liz Kresge, turned out to be our family's blessing. Liz successfully assisted each of us to gain insights about ourselves and then helped us to understand how to more effectively interact with each other. She separated the interlocked pieces of our family's emotional puzzle, threw them out on the table, and then helped us figure out how to put the pieces back together again.

In one mother-daughter therapy session, Liz said, "If I took Susan down to the other end of this hall out of your sight and pricked her with a pin, you would know, wouldn't you, Janet?"

I replied indignantly, "Of course, I'm her Mother. It's my job to know if something is hurting my daughters."

"No, Janet, that was true when Susan and Tracy were young. They are grown women now. Ever vigilant protection is no longer your job," she replied.

I was startled by her comment and felt a surge of anger. What did she know; she didn't have any children. "That's what's wrong with our world," I replied. "Mothers delegate their responsibilities and don't adequately love and protect their children. A mother's primary job is to protect her children forever."

"No, Janet. Susan and Tracy are capable of protecting themselves now," Liz replied.

I remember leaving her office feeling frustrated and confused. For days I told myself therapy was just a hoax, and Liz didn't know what the hell she was talking about. Then slowly, as my heart and my mind began to feel more receptive, I began to consider Liz's remarks more objectively. I turned her observations over and over in my mind and suddenly, days after the therapy session, I realized Liz was telling me that I had failed to give Susan and Tracy their adult wings.

I felt deeply saddened and angry with myself that I had inadvertently been repeating the same stifling mistake of earnest parental manipulation that my mother had made. I remember feeling unnerved that there were parts of myself I did not recognize nor understand. Guided by Liz's insightful and wise oversight, I felt cautiously receptive to the discovery of more insights into myself and those I loved.

During the next few therapy sessions, Liz met with my daughter Tracy, followed by a couple of solo sessions with Phil. She called shortly after meeting with Phil and Tracy and said she wanted to meet alone with me. When I arrived, she had a large poster-sized tablet and magic marker on her lap. "I want to draw a diagram for you Janet that shows the internal relationships of a functioning family" she said. Initially I could not see what she was drawing, but when she turned the tablet I saw this diagram.

"Now," Liz said, "let me draw another diagram that I believe captures the dynamics in your family." The moment Liz turned our family's diagram around and began to explain what it meant, I began to cry.

Liz carefully explained that a family's primary bond should lie between a husband and wife, with the strength of that marital relationship protecting the children's well-being. She noted that siblings should be primarily bonded to siblings, enabling them to support each other for a lifetime. She made clear that these interactive relationships lay at the heart of constructive family dynamics.

Within our family's challenging dynamics, she noted, I had, over the years, systematically built an impenetrable wall around Phil, believing that it was the only way to protect myself and our daughters from his erratic behavior. Phil, carrying a deeply scarred sense of worth stemming from a destructive childhood, recognized his inability to constructively interact with his daughters and wife. He also came to believe that the wall I had built was justified and thus he was unable to make constructive efforts to tear it down. Liz also pointed out that my primary bond, due to Susan's many physical and emotional needs, ran between myself and Susan. Phil and Tracy remained isolated and alone.

Liz pointed out that having lost my father I had never had the opportunity to see normal dynamics between a husband and wife, and that imbalanced experience had driven deep into my being the notion that loyalty and primary bonding was between a mother and her children. That childhood notion had been compounded by Phil's inability to constructively parent his daughters. Both experiences ensured my protective aggression and dominant parenting style, and Phil's sense of parental isolation. My dominant parenting style also undermined strong sibling relationships.

I could still feel the breathless impact of Liz's observations. I recalled taking the diagram home and showing it to Phil, asking if he thought it was emotionally accurate. "Absolutely," he replied. Next, I invited Tracy to lunch and shared the diagram with her. As she looked at the diagram, her chin began to quiver and her eyes filled with tears. I had Tracy's answer.

Therapeutic insights, having opened a safe emotional route to my core, shook loose two interior voices. Along with my saving rabbits instincts there was also a warrior woman waiting to be acknowledged. Having always considered myself exclusively a saver of rabbits, it was unsettling to recognize a warrior's voice, similar to my mother's, living within me. But I knew that I needed to change the way I interacted with Susan during the throes of her bulimia. I also needed to challenge Phil regarding our marital issues and use my warrior's armor to protect myself against his often hurtful incursions. *Suit up, Janet, there are both internal as well as external battles to be fought. Stop enabling and challenge demons head on, no matter the risk.*

Two battles in particular demanded I don my warrior persona to confront untenable circumstances. The first with Susan was urgent since her physical health and survival depended upon her confronting her demon and my interacting with her demon differently. The second battle, with Phil, required substantial changes in our interactions as well. Understanding that I could not do battle effectively on two fronts, I chose war with Susan's demon as my initial incursion.

Susan had asked to move home during her freshman year at F&M college, and Phil and I agreed she could do so. Bulimia drove Susan physically and emotionally, often forcing her to deceptively protect her demon. Her deceptions made me feel extremely anxious about protecting myself against her untruths while continuing to try to be supportive. I told Susan she was welcome to move home with one caveat: If I discovered that she was using our groceries to abuse herself she would be asked to leave. She agreed and moved home. I made every effort to make sure I never had bowls of food sitting out that would present a challenge for her.

Over the course of a few months, I watched as Susan's weight fluctuated. Whenever she and I would go to the grocery store together, I sensed anxiety and uneasiness in her. She explained that going to the grocery store was one of the ultimate challenges for any bulimic, like an alcoholic in a liquor store.

One morning, having invited a neighbor for tea, I filled a candy dish about ten minutes before she was scheduled to arrive. I went to the kitchen to make tea and when I went back into the living room the candy dish was empty. My warrior woman emerged with a vengeance as I climbed the stairs two at a time. I will no longer be your enabler, I said repeatedly as I tore down the hall. I flung open the bathroom door, slamming it against the tile wall. Susan, startled, looked up in dismay.

"Did you eat the candy in the dish in the living room?" I asked.

"Yes," she said.

"You have fifteen minutes to get out of my house. Fifteen. Do you understand me? Pack your suitcase and get out."

"Mother, you can't mean it. Where will I go?"

"I have never meant anything more in my life, Susan. Get out. I will no longer allow you to hurt and deceive me. I am too good a friend. I don't care where you go."

Turning, I walked as fast as I could down the hall, slammed my bedroom door, called my neighbor apologizing that a personal issue had arisen that would require me to postpone our get-together until later in the week. I climbed into bed, put a pillow over my head and sobbed myself dry.

Susan left, returning about five days later. "Mother," she said, "don't you think this is silly for you and me, who are good friends, not to be speaking to each other?"

"You don't get it, do you, Susan? Ever since your sophomore year in high school, all through your struggles at Wesleyan, then here at Franklin and Marshall, I have supported you every way I could. I have been an exquisitely good friend. But I'm through enabling you. What I have come to realize, Susan, is that I cannot save you. The only person who can save you, is you. If you destroy yourself, I am just going to have to live with it. Now please go. I can't afford to talk with you further because I am so angry that I might say something I will regret forever."

Susan left and went to live with friends. I knew where she was living and would periodically check with her friends concerning her well-being, all the while mourning.

She did take charge of her bulimic demons and went on to graduate from college, obtain a master's degree and a PhD. Years later she told me, "You are my best friend. When you gave up on me, I knew I had to take charge of my demons. You saved my life by rescuing me from college, you saved my life a second time by throwing me out of the house. When you stopped enabling me, I had to begin enabling myself. Thank you."

Quietly, I thanked the warrior woman inside me.

Having won the first skirmish, I suited up for battle a second time. Phil's unpredictable and erratic anger forced the girls and me to live as if we were suspended over fragile eggshells. Any missteps threatened to shatter the shells, tearing the delicate membrane that protected the essence of our family. Often not able to identify the source of his anger and always confused and intimidated by my inability to lovingly stabilize our lives, I tried to communicate my frustration and sorrow to Phil.

First, I tried soft, loving, saving rabbits approaches, telling him how much he is loved, encouraging him to confront the sources of his anger and fear. He usually responded by rushing into his protective cave saying, "I don't dislike people, I fear them," then rolled the largest emotional stone he could find into the entranceway.

I stood outside the cave shouting, "It is important that you confront your fears. I will try to help you understand why you find it so difficult to trust others with your heart. Please know that you are a good and loving man in spite of all your childhood abuses. Your parents were unable to love you, Phil. That does not mean you don't deserve to be loved. It means your parents lacked the capacity to love, not just you, but any child. They simply did not understand how to love."

Finally, when all else failed, I again donned my warrior's armor, crossed the moat and waged a no-holds-barred battle. I shouted, cursed, and laid down ultimatums.

"Can you hear me?" I shouted. "Hear my pain and frustration? See me imploding?"

My outbursts brought Phil cautiously out of his cave, only momentarily, and I rejoiced to see him. Unfortunately, the threatening din of my warrior's anger confirmed for Phil that family was not emotionally safe. Those encounters drove Phil deeper and more protectively inside himself.

He often said to me, "If you really knew who I am, you would not love me."

That statement left me baffled and confused. "What don't I know? What could possibly live inside you that is so dark and threatening to our relationship?" I was convinced that if we were to break the in-cave, out-of-cave, rabbit-warrior syndrome, we needed skilled, professional help.

Liz heard me as I had never been heard by Phil. She helped me to understand that my anger only served to reconfirm for Phil that family was not safe. She helped me to express my anger in more constructive ways so Phil could hear me. And Phil began to take an antidepressant to address a chemical imbalance that had never been previously diagnosed. Within a few short months, it became evident to Phil and his loved ones that the medication had begun to stabilize his emotional difficulties. Liz continued teaching both of us to listen to each other and speak in tones that the other could hear.

My thinking patterns moved from black-and-white absolutes to soft grays. Liz taught me to accept ambiguity and uncertainty. She assisted me in understanding that if I adjust myself and my interactions with others, then, in turn, others' responses will be adjusted as well.

The profound notion that the only person you can really change is yourself changed my worldview. As significantly, I gained the understanding that I am in charge of what persons and ideas I allow inside myself.

As we all grew to more fully understand our family's dynamics and deepened our understanding of each other's perspectives and emotional needs, we continued to make adjustments. With the passage of time, Liz observed that we had made substantial relational progress and suggested that we take some non-therapeutic time to absorb her counsel and further adjust our interactions with one another. Each of us visited Liz from time to time to clarify and further explore emotional issues as they arose. Because of difficult but rewarding therapeutic work, our family began to grow itself towards a loving peace we had never known before.

I was grateful to Liz Kresge for sharing her professional insights about our family. Family therapy provided new perspectives and the reparative skills necessary to nurture our family's relationships. Therapy encouraged dialogue that was based upon constructive and balanced interactions with respectful listening and responsiveness.

Marriage and family relationships are hard work requiring conscientious oversight and ongoing reparative efforts. Therapy provided the tools to reconcile differences as well as the ability to differentiate between damaging conflict and the normal day-to-day tensions of close relationships. Liz's insights along with our family's willingness to risk opening our hearts to one another made our challenging journey possible.

As I emerged from my plunge into the Cape's refreshing water, mother-daughter relationships came to mind. I thought about the similarities between Liz's analysis of the mother-daughter relationship and Nancy Friday's *My Mother, Myself* observations. Both had cautioned against symbiotic unexamined mother-daughter bonds. I had come to understand that mother-daughter relationships require constant vigilance as the relationship mutates and grows over time. Love requires ongoing and constant nurturing, vigilance, and adaptation to change if it is to remain a positive exchange.

Settling into my beach chair, I drank a Coke and ate my egg salad sandwich and chips. I slathered myself with additional sun block, put my chair into a reclining position, and closed my eyes against the sun. *Long after they are over, therapy sessions continue to reveal insights. Such was the power of Liz's therapeutic assistance. She would ask probing questions, I would give a response; she would either confirm my answer or lead me towards an alternative perspective by suggesting ways I might approach issues differently.*

Sometimes I left sessions feeling frustrated and confused, only to have helpful insights emerge days later. Sometimes I left sessions feeling exhilarated at insights gained about new ways of being. Therapy gave me the power to first know myself and then to apply that knowledge to my most significant relationships.

As I drifted into an afternoon nap wrapped in the warmth of the sun, I thought about how Liz had acknowledged the legitimacy of my warrior voice and how she had taught me to balance the warrior and the rabbit that lived together deep within my being.

I awakened to see the sun turning the sky into an artist's palette of rose, gold, and amber as it began to slip towards the edge of the sea. My favorite time at the beach, I thought. Pouring myself wine, I lifted my glass to toast the quiet beauty of this place. Finishing my wine and taking one last quick dip before darkness descended, I headed up the sandy road for home.

I thought about all the folks who say, "I don't do the therapy thing." "You should," I tell them.

Discovering ourselves, under all the layers of cultural, familial, and self-imposed restrictions is one of the most difficult but breathtakingly beautiful journeys anyone can take. The trick is to persevere until you find the right therapist for you and yours, and that search may require some false starts until you find that the fit is right.

The critically important component is the willingness of all partners to do the very difficult, emotionally exhausting work that is required, so that each person has clarity about who she or he is and what changes are necessary. Egos find this scary work, but the results are life-enhancing.

My therapeutic experience had taught me that it might take years, many trials and errors, some setbacks, and an inordinate amount of frustrated but determined love to literally save ourselves from ourselves. I remain convinced that therapy literally saved my daughter's life, my marriage, and strengthened our family's ability to love one another.

I grilled myself a cheeseburger, made a salad, and took dinner up to watch the news. Later I called Phil to make sure all was well at home. He assured me that everyone was fine. He had had dinner with Tracy, Carl and the girls the evening before, and had spoken with Susan on the phone. He had made his plane and bus reservations for the end of August and was beginning the countdown until he joined me on the Cape.

"Only four weeks left," he said.

"Yes, only four weeks left," I replied. Wishing him a goodnight and hanging up the phone, I worried about having enough time to accomplish all I had set out to accomplish. I felt a twinge of sadness that the summer was ending, but also felt exhilarated about returning to family.

"Jesus tells us in The Gospel of
Thomas that 'The kingdom will not
come by expectation. The kingdom
of the Father is spread over the earth
and men do not see it.' In other
words, bring it about in your hearts . .
. All you have to do is see it."

Joseph Campbell

CHAPTER TWENTY

A RABBIT FOR MOTHER

A gloriously sunny Cape morning awakened me. I grabbed some orange juice and toast, ran back upstairs, and propped myself up in bed to read. As I finished the last few chapters of Friday's book, more memories of Mother surged into my mind.

At 85, Mother decided that it was time to sell her Camp Hill house and enter a retirement community. She asked her friend Ethel to go with her to sign up for an apartment and then, as was her life-long pattern, she told her children that she had done so after the fact. Mother had agonized when she admitted her own parents into a retirement home, and therefore wanted to spare her children from having to make that very difficult decision.

Mother selected the furniture and decorative items she wished to take with her. The home provided a bed and dresser, so Mother chose to take a favorite large leather

lounge chair for her bedroom. For her living room, she selected a mahogany bridge table and four chairs, three wing
chairs, a rose-colored Aubusson rug, some paintings, lamps
and many family photographs. She bought a small couch
which pulled out into a single bed, saying she would have a
place for Joyce or me to sleep overnight, should we chose to
do so. We never did.

After deciding which items to take along, she arranged
for an appraiser to mark an estimated value on everything else.
On moving day, all her children and their spouses helped to
get her settled. Everyone, including her, struggled to be upbeat
during the move. Her apartment was quite charming once all
her personal things were in place, but starkly different from
magnificent Barleycroft and her lovely home on Arlington
Road.

As we drove away with Mother standing at her apartment
door waving good-bye, my heart felt like it would burst. I felt
homesick for what had been and was no longer possible. I felt
deep sorrow for my mother. I knew how difficult it must have
been for her to have given up her beautiful home and face living in a place where so many were merely waiting to die. It
did not seem possible that this vibrant, capable woman called
Mother had been transformed by life into a white-haired, almost blind, child-like figure.

Shortly after her moving day, I took Mother a gift that
I thought might bring her comfort during her transition to
retirement community living. It was a cuddly, brown stuffed
bunny rabbit with a powder blue bow. I told her she could hug
it whenever she got lonely. Then I read her my adaptation of a

story originally written by Father Martin Bell in *The Way of The Wolf* (1968) called "Barrington Bunny."

I hoped that my adapted version would ease her loneliness and strengthen her courage, and reassure her that she would never be alone. She thanked me through tear- filled eyes and told me she would keep Barrington on her bed. Whenever I went to visit, she would comment about how much she loved Barrington and what comfort he brought her.

Barrington Bunny is the story of a rabbit who never felt like he belonged with the other creatures of the forest. He always felt unloved and alone. One Christmas Eve a great snowstorm arose, and Barrington asked many forest creatures' families if they might shelter him from the storm. Each time he asked, he was told he "wasn't one of them." Finally, with the storm raging around him, alone and despondent, he heard a tiny squeak and moved towards the sound. He found a tiny mouse shivering and crying about having lost his mother.

Barrington told the little mouse to crawl under his furry belly where he would be warm and they would search together to find his mother after the storm had passed. The small mouse thanked him and nestled beneath Barrington. In the morning after the snowstorm had stopped, the small mouse's mother, searching for her baby, came upon a frozen bunny. She found her baby safely nestled beneath Barrington's fur.

My gift was intended to be a reminder to Mother that she, like Barrington, had sheltered her children from most of life's adversities as best she could. And that when she felt lonely at the retirement home, as she had felt so often in her younger years, she could hold onto Barrington to fortify her courage.

At the end of Barrington Bunny, a great silver wolf emerges from the forest to accompany Barrington's spirit home. Feeling alone and rejected by the other creatures of the forest, Barrington had made the ultimate loving sacrifice to protect one of God's creatures. Sensitive to the fragility and vulnerability of those around him, he had used his gifts of love and warmth to protect and nurture those accompanying him on his journey through the dangerous forest. Barrington was love. The silver wolf had been sent to accompany Barrington home for a job well done.

I wanted my mother to understand that with enormous courage and determination against all odds, she too had accomplished a job well-done. She was Barrington. I knew that Mother was waiting for her own great silver wolf to accompany her home.

CHAPTER TWENTY-ONE

WALKING MOTHER HOME

Arising to a gray rainy morning, I smiled, knowing a gray Cape morning permitted me to linger in my nightie and bathrobe while sipping tea in my favorite chair by the sunroom window. As I prepared my tea and toast, my eyes settled on a refrigerator magnet, one of the Christmas gifts Mother had given me the Christmas before she died. The magnet wrapped like a present and tied with a small bow had a note attached that read:

> This is a very special gift
> That you can never see
> The reason it's so special is
> It's just for you from me
> Whenever you are lonely
> Or even feeling blue
> You only have to hold this gift
> And know I think of you.

You never can unwrap it
Please leave the ribbon tied
Just hold the box close to your heart
It's filled with love inside. (Anonymous)

I removed the magnet, fighting back tears and held it close to my heart, repeating the ritual I had done so many times before. Last Christmas when I received her gift I had anxiously suspected the gift marked the formal beginning of a good-bye she knew was fast approaching.

Now, she indeed was gone. I was still wondering if I would survive her passing.

———————

Painful memories crashed into my mind as I settled by the sunroom window. In 1997, at age eighty-five, Mother was hospitalized with abdominal discomfort. With Joyce and me at her side, she made the decision not to have a grapefruit-sized abdominal aneurism repaired. She told her doctors in attendance, "I have lived a long and full life. My mission is accomplished. I have had two heart attacks and open-heart surgery. I do not intend to have any additional surgery. Whatever time I have left, I will enjoy. It is time for me to make room for the young. My mission is accomplished. I will take it as it comes." An image of Barrington Bunny stoically huddled down against the winter gale while sheltering the lost baby mouse crashed into my heart.

Joyce and I concurred that the decision was Mother's, and only Mother's, to make. However, we spoke privately with the doctors to make sure we understood the realities of her decision not to have surgical intervention to repair the aneurism. The doctors explained that Mother's age and compromised heart increased the likelihood that she might not survive the surgery. Given the size of the aneurysm, they could not predict how long Mother might survive: hours, weeks, months, even a year or two was their best guesstimate. Joyce and I let John and Joan know of Mother's circumstances.

With all of us aware of Mother's precarious health issues, we wanted to savor every family moment we had left together. So, my younger sister Joyce invited everyone to her house for a Memorial Day swimming party. Joyce and her husband, David, always included Mother in all their family holiday celebrations and vacations. Memorial Day 1999 was one of those occasions.

The holiday marked the last extended family gathering.

Except for my brother John who was on an African safari and my older sister Joan who had to undergo dialysis three days per week in her battle with diabetes, we celebrated the holiday together at Joyce's home. Enjoying delicious food and drinks, swimming in Joyce's pool, playing games and laughing together all contributed to a wonderful family gathering. But Mother appeared somewhat withdrawn and distracted.

Always the one to be in the middle of any family activities, Mother sat alone in a chair somewhat removed from the rest of the family. Her distant, aloof, reflective and pale facial expressions hinted that she was not fully engaged, but appeared to be in some other place. Then when Joyce and I began to swim laps, Mother quickly joined us. Joyce, explaining that she had just filled the pool that morning, cautioned that the water might be too cold for Mother. Mother only laughed and reminded us that swimming was one of her favorite activities.

"Remember what my father always said, that I would never amount to anything because all I ever wanted to do was go swimming," she chortled. "One thing about being eighty-seven years old, you fear nothing, least of all cold water. It feels wonderful to push physical limits, to become one with the water, floating free. I'll be just fine, don't worry."

As the day drew to an end, we all said our thanks and exchanged hugs before traveling home. Mother planned to stay at Joyce's for a few more days. Early the next morning, Mother came downstairs in her bathing suit and asked Joyce to join her for a swim. Joyce tried to dissuade her, mentioning cold-water temperatures again, but Mother persisted. They swam laps and sunned intermittently throughout the day. In the early evening, Joyce, her husband David, and Mother dined at the country club. Mother enjoyed her usual two Manhattans. When they returned to Joyce's, they retired for the night.

About 4:00 a.m. Joyce awakened to the sound of moaning coming from Mother's bedroom. She found her writhing in pain. The aneurysm had burst. Mother did not want to go to a hospital and possibly risk an intervention that might prolong her life. She begged Joyce to just sit with her and let it happen, but as the intensity of the pain increased, Joyce knew that Mother needed pain medication and professional supports she could not provide. She called an ambulance and then called me as I was dressing to go to work.

On the way to the hospital, I tried to comprehend what life would be like without Mother. I could not. My thoughts were of death and the all too familiar mourning and fear that follows in the aftermath of loved one's dying. I could feel the internal war begin. My brain's rational side was beginning to prepare me to survive another loved one's death by reminding me that following the horrendous darkness, the light inevitably returns, while the irrational side whispered that maybe, just maybe, she would somehow survive and all would be well.

How does someone who has been part of every day of your life cease to exist? Maybe she will be gone when I get to the hospital. Or, perhaps the doctors will have stabilized her, and she will be fine. Will Mother be conscious and able to talk to us? Will she change her mind and permit the surgery? Or, is it too late? As I pulled into the hospital parking lot, my heart raced and sweat began to form behind my knees; lightheadedness and the ongoing mind game continued: *Yes, she will recover; no, she will not survive.*

Walking into the emergency room, I found Joyce, her husband David, and the doctor talking with Mother about what steps might be taken to surgically repair the leaking aneurysm. Mother stood firm. "Just give me something to control the pain. I know, young man, that you have been trained to save lives, but please know that I have no intention of having surgery to repair anything. I have a living will. My body has struggled for years just to keep going, to maintain my dignity. I have lived a good life. My children are all well provided for and taken care of. My mission is accomplished."

As Mother said these words, I expected to feel panic. Instead I felt blessed numbness, a sort of suspended animation. I knew crushing sorrow would follow, but for now I welcomed the numbness that would get me through losing her.

The doctor agreed that he would hospitalize Mother and keep her comfortable. Once she was in her hospital room with Joyce and me by her side, the doctor revisited the issue one more time.

"Are you sure, Mrs. Reilly, about your decision not to surgically intervene?" he questioned.

"I have never been surer, young man. I will be fine. I have never feared death. Just keep me as comfortable as you can. Thank you for your concern. During my first heart attack as I began to lose consciousness, I felt a peace I had never known before. But I sensed that my children still needed me, so I fought to return. This time I plan to immerse myself in the beautiful music and follow the light home. The doctor took her hand saying, "Bless you, Mrs. Reilly, on your journey home."

Joyce and I each took turns calling family members to let them know Mother was indeed dying, and if they wanted a chance to say good-bye, they should come within the next few hours.

They came—every child, every grandchild, and every in-law. My brother John had just returned home from safari the day before. My sister Joan knew by her husband's expression when he picked her up after dialysis that something was wrong. When he told her Mother was dying, she insisted he immediately drive her to the hospital so she could say good-bye.

All the children and grandchildren had arrived at Mother's bedside when Joan, accompanied by her husband, walked through the door leaning on her walker. Mother's face glowed when she saw her. "Joannie, I can't believe you're here. I'm so glad to see you!"

As if her mission were truly accomplished, Mother smiled gently and closed her eyes. We would not hear her voice again.

Everyone left about an hour later, leaving Joyce and me to walk Mother home. We pulled up reclining chairs next to her bed and softly reminisced about treasured memories, reminders of loved ones who had made the same transformative journey-memories of Daddy, our step-grandmother Florence, her grandson Little John, our stepfather Tom. Eventually, we fell ever so lightly asleep, resting but hearing Mother's every breath.

When we awoke at dawn, it was clear that Mother would not survive another day. She appeared peaceful but unresponsive. Nurses came and nurses went during the day, bringing sandwiches and iced tea, which we failed to touch. We deeply appreciated their thoughtfulness towards us, and their quiet attentive caring for Mother. Phil, along with Joyce's oldest daughter, Helen Marie, stopped into Mother's room to tell us they would be in the sunroom next door if we should need them. Just knowing they were there was an enormous comfort.

Sometime, mid-afternoon, Joyce and I gathered on either side of Mother's bed and held her hands. "Mother, remember when you had your first heart attack and I was riding in the ambulance with you?" I asked her quietly. "Remember when your eyes rolled back in your head and I grabbed your cheeks shouting, come on MB, you're a warrior; I know you can beat this, don't leave us, we all need you. Come on fight, Mother? And fight you did. Your eyes re-centered and you were back. After your second heart attack and following your open heart surgery, we finally talked about what happened during that initial ambulance ride."

"You told me that you could feel yourself going down a long tunnel and could hear gorgeous music. That you wished to continue moving towards the light, but you could hear my frantic voice calling you to return. You said you felt a peace like you had never felt before and that you wanted to continue moving through the tunnel towards the light. But hearing my pleadings you knew that your mission was somehow not complete. You needed to return to family."

"Mother, your mission is truly completed now. Joyce and I are with you and we both want you to follow the light now. We will be OK, please know that. Dad is waiting for you. And Barrington Bunny's great silver wolf has emerged from the forest to take you home. Go with him 'Beeber,' we love you."

Mother had always said that I had the voice of an angel, and from the time I was little she would often say, "Sing, Blondie, sing." Sitting on her hospital bed holding her hand, I began singing "Amazing Grace." I felt in my heart that Mother could hear me as she raced through the tunnel towards the light. As I sang and looked into my sister's eyes, I knew we were both grateful that Mother's struggle was about over, while at the same time wondering if we could survive her loss.

Moments later, Mother grimaced as though she were in some discomfort. The nurses had been instructed to keep her comfortable, so I ran down the hall and told the nurse that Mother appeared to be in pain.

She came immediately to her bedside, took her vitals, looked at Joyce and me and said, "I gave her morphine a short while ago, but I suppose I could give her a bit more."

We understood what the nurse was saying. "Please do what you can to keep her from suffering," we said in unison. The nurse injected the morphine and left the room.

We continued to hold Mother's hands, talking softly to her about following the light. We knew if she believed we would be all right, she would let go.

In a matter of minutes, Mother's face lost all life. "She's gone, Joycie," I whispered. "My God, she's really gone."

I ran for the nurse, and she confirmed that indeed Mother had died.

I ran to Phil and threw my arms around him and began to sob, "MB's gone, Phil, I cannot believe it, she's really gone." Joyce spent a few moments alone with Mother's body and then came into the sunroom to get Helen, who adored her grandmother. They spent time with Mother's body saying their own good-byes. I could not bring myself to go back into her room.

My mother died at 4:45 p.m. on June 3, 1999. When I returned home, I noticed, as I walked through our foyer, that the grandfather's clock my stepfather had made for MB in his workshop at Barleycroft, and which I now owned, had stopped at exactly 4:45 p.m. Coincidence? Synchronicity? Divine? I chose to believe it was Mother's soul that wanted me to know she had heard my last song and knew Joycie and I were by her side. She seemed to be saying, "I'm home, Janet, I'm home." I said out loud to the clock, "Amazing grace indeed, Mother, amazing grace."

Interestingly, Susan later told me that as she drove home from the hospital, she had asked MB to send us a reassuring sign that she had arrived home.

Joyce and I, carrying out Mother's wishes, met with the funeral director at the local Camp Hill funeral home from which all our loved ones had been buried. She wished to be cremated and her ashes buried between her husband and grandson.

As Joyce and I drove away from the funeral home, perhaps in an attempt to break the enormous tension we felt, we began to reminisce and giggle about when the two of us went to pick up our Grandmother Della's ashes at the same funeral home. Because we had never experienced cremation before, we were both very nervous and giddy. We expected the box to be very light, but it was very heavy. We put "Della" in the backseat of our car, telling her that we were taking her to Wendy's and drove to the drive-through window for cheeseburgers and fries.

We called Mother to tell her we had picked up Della, were in the Wendy's drive-through, and would pick her up in about ten minutes for the sprinkling of Della's ashes. Mother scolded us for being disrespectful. We assured Mother that we thought, with Della's great sense of humor, she would enjoy the notion of going for fries and burgers with her two granddaughters one last time.

Shortly before Mother's funeral, I decided to go through the gray-metal strongbox she had given me when she went to the retirement home. I wanted to review her personal documents in preparation for settling her estate. When I opened the box and saw Mother's handwriting on three envelopes, I felt emotionally overwhelmed.

Just the sight of her distinctive handwriting caused my eyes to burn with tears as I looked heavenward, clutching each envelope against my heart. It felt as if, for just a few moments, she wasn't really gone. I felt as if she had given me the most beautifully unanticipated gift I had ever received.

The first envelope was addressed "To My Four Wonderful Children" and it read:

> Love so eludes definition. At times I am so power-less to express or show my feelings. Loving you more each day, it occurs to me so often, that the opportunity to tell you may not be possible in the future. I fear not being lucid; therefore, I want you to know how much I love you all. You have been my life. Without you, life would have had no purpose.
>
> My prayer is for a fast and easy death in order for you to be spared the agony of waiting and watching. I do not fear death and I am ready to meet my maker and your father. 'Thou wilt be done.'
>
> Mother

Picturing her sitting alone in her retirement living room, struggling to express the depth of her love for us, reassuring us that she had no fear of death, trying to capture in writing what she could not express to us personally, made me feel grateful for her love as well as feel a deep sadness that I would never have an opportunity to talk to her about what she had written.

As I opened the second envelope entitled "To The Children," it seemed obvious that the first letter had not sufficiently reassured her that we would grasp the enormity of her love. I wondered how much time had elapsed between the writing of the letters and in what order she had written them. This message was sheer poetry.

> Grieve not nor speak of me with tears.
> But laugh and talk of me as if I were beside you.
> I love you so. 'Twas heaven here with you.
> MB

I was left breathless and in tears by the beauty of Mother's poetic message, her effort to document her love for us. I read it over and over again until I had driven it into the deepest recesses of my heart, there to remain, as she had intended, as a source of comfort and strength.

The last letter addressed "To My Children" read:

> The barrier I built around myself will never completely dissolve. I have forced myself to realize that I am not that different from other people. Failing to realize that others are going through hell can make me a little selfish. It is difficult for me to share my emotions—few people know me as I really am, and

even with myself I am moody, different every day. All my life, I have yearned for someone I could depend on. It is silly to have the feeling of dependency, but all my life I have felt that need. I never found it in my mother—never trusted my father. Those who gave me a feeling of dependency were taken. As a result, I feel so alone. My children were cherished and the only thing I ever had that loved me and really depended on me. I loved each one and was so blessed to have them, but now they are gone which is the natural and right thing.

The journey is very near the end and I am recognizing eagerness. I end by telling myself I had few accomplishments and, were I to have the opportunity to do it again, I would not know how to improve the process.

To those who would be interested in knowing just a part of me.

This third letter provided insights into the adult woman who was my mother. I felt an overwhelming sadness that she had found it impossible to express, as an adult woman to her adult children, who she really was.

Over the years, Mother had shared small glimpses into her childhood and young adulthood, glimpses that resurfaced in my mind as I struggled to understand what she was saying in her third letter. She spoke of emotional barriers, of distrust and loneliness, created by an erratic and painful childhood that had left her locked behind walls she could not tear down, not even for her beloved children.

My mother had a desperate need to belong to someone. She had suffered irreparable damage when her mother deserted her at age twelve. That harm was compounded by being left in the care of an embittered and publicly humiliated father whose rage and frustration blinded him to his daughter's emotional needs.

Over the years, Mother had shared moments about this excruciatingly lonely time in her life. She told me of returning from school one day and for the first time not being met at the end of the lane by her beloved dog, Buddy. Repeatedly calling her beloved dog's name, her father finally emerged from the barn to announce that he had shot the dog because "he was a nuisance and of no use to anyone."

Her father had been raised on a farm and had little schooling. He ran a dairy for many years when Mother was young. After her mother left, and a public divorce decree emblazoned with a large red "A" added to Mother's shame and confusion, her father determined to put his marriage and the dairy that reminded him of his wife behind him. He established a successful contracting company. My mother always alluded to how grateful she was to her father for "sticking with her" after the divorce. I remember thinking her gratitude was puzzling. *What father would turn his back on his only child? How could she continue to care for a father who never hesitated to remind her that "if you were only a boy, I would give you anything."*

Suddenly, an additional piece of magical thinking shattered as I recalled another traumatic Barleycroft incident that

I experienced as a young adult. Having finished a swim in the lake, I had walked through the meadow toweling off my hair and had quietly entered the glass-enclosed sunroom off the kitchen. I could hear loud and angry voices. My mother and grandfather were in the throes of yet another heated argument. As if to deliver the death blow of the battle, my grandfather shouted, "I've said it before and I'll say it again, you're just like your mother who ran off with the hired hand. You have no loyalty, no respect. And furthermore, I have always suspected that you are not even my daughter."

I stood stunned by the viciousness of his attack and felt rage erupting deep inside. Mother stood silently immobilized. The battle had been won. My grandfather's lethal thrust had inflicted the intended damage to his opponent's heart. He had crippled his foe.

I had witnessed my grandfather's "no-holds-barred" warfare before. His ego had never recovered from the public humiliation of his wife's desertion. He grasped every opportunity to seek revenge against his wife through my mother. My grandfather could be a vicious combatant.

Not being able to contain my rage at his abuse of my mother, I stomped into the kitchen erupting with venomous outrage. "What kind of a man are you? Didn't you punish my grandmother enough by labeling her an adulterer in front of the whole world? Wasn't that sufficient to assuage your male ego? Do you have to continue to punish your only child for events over which she had no control? Evil flows from you. Your inability to forgive your wife for an indiscretion that occurred so many years ago poisons your life. May God forgive you for attempting to continue to break your daughter's heart. She didn't create your problems, you did. Own them and give her the respect and love she so deserves!"

As I stomped from the room, I recalled Mother sharing a childhood story about looking out the window as a young girl as her mother flirted with the hired hand. She felt shame that her father did not know what was going on and knew she would never tell him. She feared for her mother if he should find out. And feared for herself should her mother decide she wanted to remain with this stranger.

Her worst fears came to fruition. Her mother deserted her with no word of how she could be reached, leaving Mother in the care of a desperately bitter father and a community that self-righteously meted out shame, not only to the divorced parents, but their children as well. Mother spoke of her schoolmates stoning the backs of her feet and legs as she walked home from school, and how she agonized about what she had done wrong.

I knew devastation at twelve years of age when I lost my father. And he had not chosen to leave me. I often thought about how Mother must have felt when her mother consciously chose to desert her; how she felt as the one left in the care of a man her mother could no longer stand to live with. Children abandoned by a parent blame themselves for somehow being responsible. Her father's public declaration of adultery and the resultant red "A" splashed across the divorce decree only compounded her anguish. The scar tissue that formed in her twelve-year-old being never healed, and created an insatiable sense of homesickness and loneliness that would haunt my mother throughout her life.

Following the divorce, Mother, who was determined not to remain trapped keeping house for her father until he found another spouse, began to think about how best to take charge of her own life. She had often heard her mother lament being trapped by her own lack of education. Mother decided that education held the key to her freedom and her future. She pleaded and cajoled her father into attending prep school and college. She battled to justify the expense each time the tuition came due and each time her father argued, "If you were only a boy I'd give you anything, but educating a woman is a waste." Mother finally won the battle. Ironically, years later, my grandfather met and married an elementary school teacher. I suspect that was mere happenstance, not any shift in his perspective about the value of educating women.

Education did indeed hold the keys to Mother's future. Shortly before graduating from The University of Pennsylvania's dental hygiene school, she met my dad. Her determined striving for an applicable education would, years later, prove to be essential to the survival of our family.

When my father and mother met on a blind date, my father was sharing a dental practice with his father. In time, Mother convinced Dad that they should move from Philadelphia to the Harrisburg area to set up his own dental practice. Double ironies—my mother, in spite of her tragic childhood, was always homesick. She had said often, "Homesick for what, I was never sure." My grandfather was delighted with his newly-acquired "son," and presented him with a down payment for a house with a dental office attached. As Mother said, "My father finally had the son he always wanted. In the eyes of my father, his son-in-law could do no wrong."

By the time my parents were married in Saint Patrick's Cathedral in Harrisburg, Pennsylvania, my mother's mother had returned to the area and was living with her parents. Much to my grandfather's chagrin, she was in attendance at my parents' wedding. Mother never found out why her mother had decided to return from Canada. In spite of the charge of adultery and the desertion of her child, my great-grandparents took her back into their home until she could find a job and an apartment. And my mother took her mother back into her heart. My grandfather's heart, or maybe just his ego, never healed.

As I remember my mother's stories about this period in her life, I am awed by the forgiveness she demonstrated towards her mother. She took her mother back into her married life, and those who did not know about the broken relationship would never have known that her mother had deserted her. Mother welcomed her mother, as well as her friends, into her home as if the abandonment had never happened. My grandmother vacationed with us, took care of us when Mother and Dad traveled, and spent holidays with us.

I suspect my mother needed to reassure herself that her mother really did care about her. Desertion by one's mother, even for a limited time, creates an overwhelming black hole of vulnerability, loneliness, unworthiness and distrust that the child carries for the rest of its life. My mother was such a child. Her four children partially filled the void, but her overwhelming sense of loneliness was bottomless. I do suspect that over time my mother grew to understand why her mother, an exquisitely young, beautiful, passionate woman, had chosen to abandon the cold, stern, controlling man she had married. But the abandonment scars formed in my mother's heart were permanent.

As all these stories Mother had shared re-emerged into my consciousness, I more fully understood what she was trying to tell her children in her third letter. I decided that I would make copies of all of her letters for my sisters and brother, but would only read the first two at her burial service. The third letter would remain exclusively for her children.

At the graveside service, our minister, Father Hoyt, spoke about the remarkable woman and strong mother she had been.

"Your mother's entire world was her family. What a perfect ending to a life devoted to family. It seems so right that your mother had a final opportunity to see each of her children and grandchildren before she died—a perfect ending for a remarkable woman. She led a memorable life, for she was a woman with exceptional qualities. Her life story reads like a great romance—filled with courage, daring, determination, beautiful people and lovely surroundings. But most important, Martel's life story must be catalogued with the great comedies. Comedies in the classic sense, that when you get to the end, you do not weep in sad recognition and empathy, not even self pity, but rather you smile and shout Alleluia . . . her mission is accomplished. She's not here, folks, she has risen! Death is but the putting out of the candle because the heavenly dawn has come. Alleluia."

As the minister compared my mother's life to classic comedy, I thought, "What a strange word to use at a funeral, a "comedy." But immediately my mind recalled Dante Alighieri's *Divine Comedy*, the epic-narrative Renaissance poem about the human spirit's struggle to move from hell's sorrow and despair towards heaven's redemptive truth and love. Truly MB's life has been a classic comedy, I thought. *My mother's life had been an ongoing battle to overcome the hell of loneliness, sorrow and despair.* I pray that she has found Dante's ninth Heaven, where all longing and discontent disappear, having been replaced by "the Love that moves the sun and all the stars."

I read Mother's two letters and distributed copies of all three to my brother and sisters. Standing, holding onto her walker, Joan began to sob. I moved through the gathering to her side, slipped my arm around her waist, and handed her a handkerchief. Through all the losses, all the hardships of our lives, I had rarely seen my sister Joan cry. Mother and Joan had had a complicated and conflicted relationship, so I thought her tears were tears tainted with some regrets. I would learn some seven months later that they were, in fact, tears of joy.

Some weeks after Mother's funeral, I sat down to further ponder the third letter she had left for us, the one I had not read publicly at her funeral. As I sat reading the letter, I wept until I could hardly breathe, and as I wept, I realized what a profoundly wonderful gift our mother had left to us, a peek into her soul. Mixed, amidst the gratitude I felt for her thoughtful gift, I felt a deep sadness that she had not sufficiently trusted her children to be able to share her overwhelming loneliness while she was still alive. It would have blessed us to have been given the opportunity to know her as an adult woman who struggled with her own pockets of darkness. It also saddened me that my mother never realized the power of her many accomplishments.

In the days that followed, I returned to her third letter many times, trying to more fully grasp the complexities of this remarkable woman's life. Each time I read it, I felt a deep sadness. Mother's emotional barriers, of distrust and loneliness created by an erratic and painful childhood, left her locked behind emotional walls she could not tear down. I came to realize that Mother had insisted that she and Dad have four children so her life would never be devoid of love again. After my father's death, she drew us to her with a stifling intensity.

As the years passed, and her children became immersed in their own families, her loneliness, driven by a sense that her children had deserted her, returned with a vengeance in her elder years. Feeling threatened and alone again, she succumbed to strident and caustic interactions with those she loved. I mourn that she was unable to open windows into her real adult being so her children could have more comfortably reassured her of what a remarkably accomplished and loving Mother she had been.

Her letter also speaks of her mood being different every day, missed opportunities, lack of accomplishment, longing for parents she could trust and depend upon, but finding none, building walls between herself and others, and not letting others know her. Tragically, this is the voice of an adult woman I did not know. I wish she had allowed me to know just a part of her, to have had the opportunity to know the real woman behind the mask. That knowing would have enriched both her life and the lives of all her children and grandchildren. Instead, her stridency often confused and alienated us, ironically compounding her sense of isolation and loneliness.

As I sat looking towards the bay, a sliver of sun broke through the clouds, reminding me that both rain and fog are essential forces on life's journey. No matter how gray the moment, the sun will return.

I thought about how important it is to understand your mother's legacy; her legacy is critical to understanding yourself. At the end of my mother's life, she chose to write short notes to provide minimal glimpses of who she was. I wished so desperately that she had written more extensively. Reading her notes and thinking about the preciousness of insights they provided, I promised myself that someday I would write about who I am as an adult woman in the context of my life's experiences and relationships, hoping that my daughters and my grandchildren will more fully know me, and thus more fully understand themselves.

CHAPTER TWENTY-TWO

ATTENDING MY
PARENTS' WEDDING

Following Mother's death, I experienced a disorienting numbness. I would sit in my car outside her retirement apartment, picturing her sitting in a patio lawn chair, her face turned towards the sun, waiting for me to visit. I would drive past my childhood home and past the farm. I would sit outside her last home on Arlington Road looking at the flowering cherry tree and wrought-iron gate, a gate she treasured because it had been made especially for her by a friend.

I thought about all the family dinners, parties, and laughter shared. I also thought about some of the sad times: Mother's first heart attack; her recovery from a second heart attack and open heart surgery; my stepfather Tommy's death; confrontations between us when she elected to make hurtfully invasive comments. Working in Harrisburg allowed me to visit her grave every lunch hour for many months. I could not believe she was really gone forever.

One noon hour, struggling to right myself, I decided to walk along the Susquehanna River and across the Walnut Street Bridge to City Island, where my mother and grand-

mother had often taken me swimming in my youth. As I left
my office at the Department of Public Welfare and crossed 3rd
Street, I began to sob uncontrollably. Stopping to catch my
breath, I looked up and found myself in front of a church.
I decided to go in to sit for a while, hoping my spirit would
find some solace. As I climbed the stone stairs, pushed open
the front door and stepped inside I saw the words, "Welcome
to Saint Patrick's Cathedral." How ironic, I thought, that the
Catholic Church might finally offer sanctuary from my pain.

I moved quietly down the center aisle trying not to dis-
turb a cluster of folks who were kneeling in prayer towards the
rear of the church. As I passed the confessional and saw the
Stations of the Cross, sweet childhood memories of attending
Mass at Good Shepherd Catholic Church safely nestled among
family, flashed across my mind. Mass was said in Latin then so
I never truly understood what the ritual was all about. Amidst
the gold-lamé copes, Christ-embellished crosses, incense, wa-
fers and wine, was what I treasured: a sense of safety and love
within family. Even today, the smell of Prince Machiabelli perfume or Old Spice aftershave instantly transport me back to a
time when my precious parents filled my world with unconditional love.

As I slowly walked towards the front of the church, my
mind's eye recalled my mother's dark exotic beauty as we sat
together in another church so very long ago. Her flashing black
eyes appeared radiant under the brim of one of her beautifully
flamboyant hats. My favorite was a large, brilliant green felt
one with a wide brim of multi-colored pheasant feathers. As a
child, I thought she looked like an Egyptian empress crowned

with iridescent jewels. When I looked at my dad sitting next to us in the pew, his handsome Irish face aglow, I knew he thought so, too.

For Christmas Dad always bought Mother a new hat for his beautiful "Babes," along with a bottle of Prince Matcha-belli perfume. The bottle he gave my mother the Christmas before he died still sits on my dressing room table. Some days when I look at the bottle I feel warmth and joy. Other days an overwhelming sense of aloneness and sadness fills my heart, reminding me that some losses hurt forever, and that we simply learn to live with broken hearts.

Memories of a secure, happy time, generated by the ca-thedral's familiar sights and smells, had momentarily broken the intensity of my mourning. As I quietly slid into the front pew, I felt the peace and beauty of my surroundings slowly seeping into my soul. I breathed deeply and expansively.

"If you are there, God," I said, "show me how best to qui-et my soul, for it feels like a bottomless river of anguish rages through me, carving a chasm into the very center of my being. Life has been transformed so profoundly that I fear I will never find peace, find me. I feel so desperately, overwhelmingly lost."

And into my anguished mind a voice whispered, "Open the hymnal in front of you, Janet, and read the words of "Amazing Grace" out loud. You sang them as your last gift to your mother; read the words again to remind yourself that grace has indeed carried her home to your dad. There is no place she would rather be." As I read, "Through many dangers, toils and snares, I have already come. Tis grace that brought me safe thus far, And grace will lead me home," I knew that my mother was home.

As I read, through tears, the words on the back of the Bishop's chair "Love Life and Do Good, I Am The Resurrection and The Life," a thundering revelation crashed into my mind. "Dear God!" I am sitting in the cathedral where Mother and Dad were married. Call it synchronicity; call it my parents' spirits reaching out to quiet my heart. My spirit soared. I felt so comforted knowing I was sitting in this magnificent cathedral, where my parents had begun their life together. I turned in my pew to picture my mother walking down the aisle in her lace-gown with long train and tulle-veil trailing behind her, her dark dramatically handsome features glowing under cascading ebony hair, eyes focused on "the most handsome man" she had ever met—one of the happiest days in my mother's life, I was sure.

At the altar, I saw my wavy-black-haired, icy-green eyed, Irish father waiting for his beloved "Babes." My parents, nicknamed, Babes and Pretty Doc, seemed so real it felt like I was a guest at their wedding. Waves of overwhelming joy and utterly desperate longing filled my heart.

I left the pew and went into an adjoining small room. At the font of holy water, I dipped my fingers, then crossed myself, something I had not done since leaving the Catholic faith shortly after my father's death so many years ago.

I never made it to the river nor to the island that day. As I walked back to the office, I felt a sense of wonderment at having been led into that holy place. I felt as if I had been led to that church to quiet my soul. I walked back to the cathedral many times over the course of the next few months, so I could feel my parents' presence and immerse myself in holy memories.

CHAPTER TWENTY-THREE

THE LOST RABBIT

G radually healing from Mother's death only months before, I turned my full attention to Joannie. Slowly, two separate bits of information I had not yet connected began to emerge within my mind: Mother's comment that her greatest fear was that one of her children would die before she did and Joan's comment, "I am so comforted by the doctor's assurances that should I choose to withdraw from dialysis I would be gone within a week to ten days."

Suddenly, I realized that my sister had been holding on to life so my mother would not have to endure her worse nightmare, the death of a child. "My God," I cried out loud. I had misinterpreted Joan's tears at Mother's funeral. Her tears were not tears of regret about unresolved mother-daughter issues; they were tears of relief and joy. With Mother gone, Joan knew she was now free to make the decision to withdraw herself from dialysis whenever she chose to do so.

A part of me fully understood that Joan had lost all quality of life. Another part of me wanted so desperately to add enough laughter and companionship to provide her with a reason to embrace life again. I questioned how I would sustain myself in a world so diminished by the loss of two of my most significant female soul-mates.

I knew in my heart, of course, that I had no right to complicate Joan's struggle by not supporting whatever decision she made. Somewhere deep inside, a steel vice tightened around my chest and abdomen, making it difficult to breathe. As in so many other instances in my life, my mind began to look for a safe place to hide.

Instead, what emerged was a vision of being trapped in an endlessly long dark valley with no ability to reach the light on the mountaintop. I tried to force myself to focus on my job as a Special Assistant to the Secretary of Public Welfare. However, every moment at work felt like precious time wasted. Feeling desperate one afternoon, I closed my office door, placed my head upon my desk and wailed myself towards the conclusion that I needed to retire. It was the only way I could spend time each day with Joan as she struggled to finalize her decision.

I gave a month's retirement notice to the Secretary of Public Welfare and the Governor.

Spending more time with Joan, I grew to fully understand the intensity of her physical and emotional hardships. Diabetes had stolen her ability to see and thus robbed her of her love of reading. Diabetes had stolen her feet through two major amputations, and thus robbed her of her ability to swim and hike. Diabetes had stolen her dark exotic beauty and vibrancy that never failed to light up a room when she entered. I was grateful that her inability to see prevented her from fully realizing the extent to which this disease had destroyed her beauty.

Diabetes had even robbed her of the ability to control her bowels and bladder. Yet even this indignity she endured without complaint.

My younger sister Joyce and I had invited Joan to lunch shortly after my retirement. On the return drive home, the car filled with an overwhelmingly sour smell. In the rearview mirror, I glanced at my sister Joyce. We both shrugged, suspecting that Joan was the source. As I assisted her up the stairs, I saw the bowel leakage all over the back of her slacks. I felt like screaming, "On top of everything else, she is expected to endure this ultimate indignity as well. It's too damn much!" Instead, I gently took her arm, telling her that she had soiled her slacks. She stoically replied, "Oh. I'll take care of it when I get inside." I marveled at her ability to tolerate such humiliating adversity with so much dignity and grace.

Once inside, I offered to assist her in cleaning herself, since I knew she could not see well enough to wash and change her slacks. Being an extremely private person, Joan assured me she would be fine without my help. She left the bathroom door open, and I watched as she struggled to remove her soiled clothes and wash herself. I wanted so desperately to help her, but I knew that would just add to her humiliation. I waited quietly in the hallway hoping she could manage to change herself. She emerged from the bathroom, moved to her bedroom and then into the living room, soiling anything she sat upon. I panicked, not knowing how best to help without humiliating her further.

Out of nowhere her husband, Hersh, appeared to take charge, assuring me that he had been assisting with clean-up for some time. As he gathered up the soiled bedspread and clothes, I grabbed rags, disinfectant and a bucket to clean the bathroom. On my hands and knees cleaning, a screaming voice inside my head shouted, "Damn you for doing this to one of your angels." And then the voice said, "There is no one to blame, Janet, God doesn't do these things."

Lacking faith in God's inclination to intervene directly in earthly matters, my angst and terror multiplied. Philosopher Joseph Campbell's observation that "death is the norm and life is the exception" kept surfacing in my mind. Many of life's experiences had certainly proven the validity of his statement.

Janet, I thought, *accept that there is no one to blame, no place to direct your rage. It's just life. Death is an integral part of life.*

Every day you get out of bed and are able to function is a mini-miracle. The human body is fragile. Rejoice in every day and all those you love, for that is all you have . . . today. No one ever promised you tomorrow.

I felt lightheaded and nauseous, overwhelmed with my sister's vulnerability, but grateful to my brother-in-law for never complaining about the level of care he was providing. And, most importantly, protecting what was left of her dignity.

As I finished scrubbing the bathroom, I recalled an ironic conversation I had had with Joan when she was hospitalized for an amputation. Hersh and I were standing in the corridor outside her room waiting for her to awaken when I asked, "Why won't she take hold of her diabetes? Can't you make her exercise and eat right? At the very least, can't you make her stop smoking? My God, she's killing herself with her denial."

Hersh replied, with resignation on his face, "I can no longer reach her. I cannot do anything right as far as Joan is concerned. I have tried."

I was sitting alone on Joan's bed when she opened her eyes and smiled. I asked her if she were in a lot of pain. She replied, "No, I have no pain." At that moment I realized the disease had done such extensive damage to her nerve endings that she could not feel pain.

Taking her hand as I sat gently next to her on the bed, I said, "I'm glad, Joannie, that you are not suffering. But I have to talk with you about taking charge of your diabetes. Why won't you do what is necessary to save yourself? Surely the doctors have told you what you must do to keep the diabetes under control. I know you are eating all the wrong things, not exercising as you should, and you continue to smoke. I have told you what Carl told me, 'if she continues to smoke I guarantee that she will end up with amputations.' And here you are. I don't understand. Do you want to die?"

She looked at me defiantly and said, "That's because the damn doctors don't know what the hell they're talking about. You remember, Mother always said 'doctors were more interested in your pocketbook than your health' and I'm convinced Mother was right. They certainly didn't save our father, now did they? Besides, I know I don't have diabetes."

I sat in stunned disbelief, and asked, "Joannie, sweetheart, then explain to me why you are lying in this hospital bed recovering from a second amputation. Why do you think you have lost another foot? What do you think is going on? The doctors have been forced to cut away parts of your body, piece by piece.

My God, you do have diabetes and it is slowly killing you. Please, please acknowledge and take charge of your disease. I will try to help you understand the disease better, but you must accept your diagnosis. Please." She simply smiled, said it would be all right and began to talk about her daughter Martel coming for a visit that evening.

In the dark cavernous folds of my heart, I began to understand that Joannie was lost. I wondered if the disease had stolen her mental capacity to recognize her plight. Since most of her visible body parts had been affected, I had to assume that the blood supply to her brain and neuron capacity were being compromised as well. Her disease had locked her into an irreversible hell. At one time Joan had a choice, but now she had none; it was too late. My heart railed against living life without her as my special friend.

As I drove home that afternoon, I recalled stories about Joan when she was a small child. How if anyone would try to force her to do something she did not want to do, she would spit over her shoulder and say, "Well, we'll see about that; that's on the next page." Being strong-willed can be an asset under certain of life's circumstances or strong-willed can lock one into blind spots that damage the ability to grapple with obvious realities. I realized that no one could save Joan. She did not have the will to save herself.

Four months after Mother's death in June, Joan entered a nursing facility not far from her home. Hersh had become unable to meet her accumulating needs. As I walked through the door for my first visit, I recalled visits with both my 90-year-old grandparents in just such a nursing facility and the emotional challenges those death watch visits brought. Since Joannie was only 63 years old, the rational side of my brain struggled to accept that she too was waiting to die. *"No, there must be a mistake. How could this golden skinned, black-haired, vital woman, three years my senior be condemned to live out her last months among the infirmed and elderly? These elderly folks have lived full lives, she has not. It's just not right."*

My sense of time had been turned upside down. I felt the power of time with the passage of every second . . . of every minute . . . of every day. Time felt like an overwhelmingly precious gift that is temporarily given, but eventually snatched back. I wanted to beg God to stop time so I could share more moments with my sister, but I knew God would not hear me. I knew that death was on the march again and nothing would hold back its deadly consequences. Once again, my task was to bring as much support and love as I could muster to a loved one who was dying. I simply had to face that reality.

I found Joan eating in the dining room with her husband Hersh, who stopped by to have dinner, as he did, each evening. I stood in the doorway leaning against the doorframe for support, with her nickname "Black Beauty" running through my mind and taking deep breaths to calm my pounding heart. "I cannot add to her anguish. I cannot," I said repeatedly, as I prepared myself to join them.

Sitting in her wheelchair smiling and laughing with those around her, Joan appeared more like a staff person who had temporarily seated herself in an empty wheelchair, merely dropping by for a chat with those for whom she cared. Her dark, shiny-short-cropped hair glowed in the candlelight. It was only when I drew up a chair to join their table that her frailty and vulnerabilities became obvious. Black Beauty was almost home.

A few days later, her daughter and I were visiting when Joan asked if we could help her into the wheelchair. "I want to go into my bedroom so I can give some things to Martel," she said. As Joan reached into the back of her closet, Martel and I exchanged quick glances, recognizing that neither of us could sustain our stoic stance for long. "Just for safe keeping," Joannie said. "You know, I really should not have brought the jewelry here in the first place. It will be safe with Martel."

The three of us returned to her living room and tried to continue casual conversation about Martel's plans for later that afternoon. When we were unable to stoically sustain ourselves any longer, Martel and I left together, promising to return soon. Once outside, we hugged each other good-bye, but could not speak.

On the way home, I pulled my car over to the side of the road, put my head down on the steering wheel and cried myself breathless. I knew I had just come one step, one moment closer, to losing my sister. Joannie was incrementally inching herself toward death, all the while helping those who loved her to understand it was time to let her go. There was still a part of me that believed she simply would not die. Irrational, yes, but I felt grateful that some distorted measure of hope remained to assist in easing me slowly into the harsh reality of another loved one dying.

On one visit, Joan was not in her apartment, and the staff informed me that she was out riding with her daughter. As I sat alone in her living room waiting for her to return, I could hear her laughter, see her breathtaking smile as she glowed, radiating joy from the simple pleasures in her life: spending time with a husband, children and grandchildren who loved her, awaiting the arrival of monthly selections from her two book clubs so she could read into the early hours of the night, spending time at her cabin in the woods, driving to Benders Restaurant to have breakfast with friends. I tried to imagine the despair she must feel when alone, trapped in this alien institutional setting, surrounded by the elderly engaged in their end-of-life struggles.

How ironic that Joannie had volunteered many hours at the Mennonite Home helping to pack up and deliver Meals On Wheels and spending time with the residents whose families came infrequently or not at all. She could hardly have imagined that not many years after her own volunteer efforts, she too would require special institutionalized care as well.

Suddenly, feeling overwhelmed with sadness, I leaped from her chair, ran down the hall, and threw open the front doors so I could feel the sunshine on my face. I sat down in a rocking chair by the front door to wait. Soon Martel drove up, hopped out of the car and began setting up her mother's wheelchair. I ran to help. Pushing Joan's wheelchair towards the front door, I began to banter with her about my coming for a visit and her not being home. "Out running around the county as soon as my back is turned," I laughingly reprimanded. When she didn't jokingly respond, a squeezing anxiety erupted deep within my being. I battled my instincts to run. *Run, hide, anywhere.* I could feel hope draining from my soul. *No way to stop*

time. No way to deny reality. My legs shook. My heart pounded.
No this cannot be happening.

I pushed her wheelchair into her room and helped her
settle into her chair. "Janet, please sit down. I need to talk with
you." I felt like the floor beneath my feet was falling away and I
was hurtling into a black crevasse. "I've decided to quit, Janet,"
I heard her say. I wanted to scream and tell her she could not
do that because I could not live without her in my life. Instead,
I sat silently for a moment trying to quell the exploding nausea
and overwhelming fear that threatened to blow a hole in my
heart. I knew one of the last gifts I could give to my beloved
sister was strong and stoic support for the decision she had
made. I had to honor her by doing this Joannie's way. I heard
my voice say from some far away place, "Joannie, I know how
tough your struggle has been. I will support your decision as
best I can."

We had a cursory conversation about what quitting
meant. She planned to refuse any more dialysis, and she had
been assured that it would be only a matter of five to seven
days. Wanting to spend every precious moment I could with
her without crowding out the special time for other family
members, I decided that I would come every day and stay as
long as I felt I was bringing her some comfort. But right then
I needed time to myself to assimilate Joan's decision to quit. I
gave her a hug with the promise that I would be back early the
next morning.

Driving home, I felt as if my hands were tied behind my
back, watching my sister teetering on a skyscraper's forty-fifth
floor ledge. I knew if I begged her not to jump, to reconsider

her decision, I would be asking her to continue to endure un-
speakable physical suffering and additional psychological humiliation. The only option I had left open to me was to ensure
that she knew how much I loved her. She had begun her journey home to be with Mother and Dad. I needed to accept that
journey, for her, as well as for myself.

I thought about never hearing Joan express self-pity, never
asking, "Why me?" She had lived her entire life with enormous grace and dignity, always nurturing with abundant love
and support all those she cherished, asking so little for herself.
Her courage never wavered and her grace continued to bless all
those who came to say good-bye.

I lay awake all that night, suspecting that she, too, was
awake, and I hoped that she could sense me by her side.

"Women, do not worry about tomorrow. Even when daylight is long in coming, the sun remembers its place in the sky. Take this blue shawl of knowledge and wrap it around your daughters, tell them that women must not be afraid to be warriors."

Nancy Wood

(Excerpt from poem in
SPIRIT WALKER, pg. 24)

CHAPTER TWENTY-FOUR

FAMILY COLLAGE

*J*oan was dressed and sitting in a chair when I arrived at her apartment the next morning. Having been robbed of her sight years ago, I announced my presence by saying, "Morning, sweet sister. I brought you a surprise, a family collage Joyce made for Mother when she moved to the nursing home. It's large, Joannie, probably twenty-by-thirty inches in size, framed in shiny gold. Black and white photos of four generations—parents, siblings, grandparents, great-grandparents, friends and neighbors-all trimmed into jigsaw-like puzzle pieces so they fit snuggly together. I will remove the picture from the wall and hang the collage directly across from your chair."

Joan's face filled with joy. "What a wonderful gift, Janet. I will know that all those I loved and who loved me are keeping me company. Thank you, thank you for bringing it for me, an especially precious gift."

I described each picture—who and where and when each picture was taken, what people were wearing, their facial expressions, overall demeanors, and their approximate ages.

So began one of the most blessed days I had ever spent with my sister. The day was filled with reminiscences of loved ones and the joys we had shared together. The unspoken truth that hung between us was most of those loved ones in the collage had already preceded Joannie in death. My hope was that she would be comforted on her own journey by being reminded of what Mother had said so often: "I go before you to prepare the path."

"Janet, do you remember the time on Arlington Road, after Dad died, when you fought with Mother, Della and Marti on behalf of Hersh and me?"

I was stunned she remembered an event from so many years ago, one that I had completely forgotten.

"Well, I do," Joan replied. "I had come home from a date with Hersh, and the ladies, sitting around the dining room table drinking heavily, announced that I was 'wasting my treasure on this man.' Rather than confront them, I ran upstairs to bed, pulled the pillow over my head and began to sob. I thought you were sleeping soundly. The next thing I knew you jumped out of bed, lunged down the steps and shouted, 'Why don't you leave my sister alone? She has done nothing wrong in loving this man. Stop judging her. Stop demeaning her decisions and the man she loves. How dare you!' There was total silence in the room. Then, you ran up the stairs as fast as you had descended, jumped back in bed, told me it would be all right. We never spoke of it again. I want you to know that I have always carried your love and kindness in my heart. You have always defended me, Janet. You've always been there for me. You have been a dear sister and friend."

We had come from a family uncomfortable with demonstrative affection, so knowing Joan knew how much I had always loved her brought me great joy. A voice inside my head whispered, *"When she lies dying she will carry the knowledge of my love in her heart, and that love will accompany her on her journey home."* I wondered if the inner voice I heard was my soul speaking to hers. I thought about how wonderful it would be, if when a loved one dies, our soul could temporarily fly next to theirs, providing a wind beneath their wings until they arrived home safely. My eyes filled with tears at the image of my soul flying in tandem next to hers.

I described one of the collage photos, a photo of my grandmother Della and her dear friend Marti laughing together as they stood in the backyard at 24th Street surrounded by gardens filled with peonies and irises. Both with their hair in buns on top of their heads. Both wearing black and silver glasses. "They almost look like sisters," I giggled.

After describing another picture of Della and Marti standing in front of the lake at Pine Grove where my family and I often went when we were young, I asked Joan, "Isn't it amazing that you ended up owning a cabin almost 50 years later by the same beach and same lake Della and Marti are standing in front of in the photo?"

"Life has a way of returning full circle," Joan replied.

Sighing deeply, she continued. "And while we are on the subject of Della and Marti, did you know they were lesbians?"

"Good Lord, no. Where did you get that idea?"

"Joyce told me some time ago that she and Mother had been walking through the foyer at 24th Street and saw them kissing with their arms wrapped around each other. Mother was furious that they had been so indiscreet."

"Well, maybe that explains why they spent so much time together—working together, taking vacations together, why Marti's marriage only lasted a matter of months, and maybe it also explains why Della ran away from her own marriage many years before," I replied. "Can you imagine being married to our cold, often times cruel grandfather, while at the same time struggling with emotional issues that that generation never acknowledged? Do you remember the stories about our severe German Lutheran great-grandfather who berated his wife Lizzy and then fell to his knees begging for forgiveness? How he read the Bible to the family every night, particularly focusing on the wrathful Old Testament God. Can you imagine how Della, fearing her parents and God's wrath, struggled to repress instincts she did not understand?"

"Nowhere to turn, Joannie, nowhere to seek solace nor advice for a lesbian woman of that generation. Not even books or magazine articles that could help you understand your struggle. Gosh, Joan, it makes me feel empathy for Della rather than rage for deserting our mother. I recall a heated conversation I had one evening with Della and shouting at her, 'I can understand running away from your cold and controlling husband, but I will never forgive you for deserting my mother. Your desertion left permanent scars on her heart. I would never desert my children, no matter what!'"

"Della shouted back at me, as I ran across the street to get in my car, 'You are young, you don't understand. Wait until you have lived awhile and you will cease to judge so harshly.'

She was right, Joan. Judging harshly is a youthful instinct born of inexperience and arrogance. Time bends and rearranges us. It teaches us that life's challenges are never simple, always complex. In time, we come to understand there are no definitive answers, just perplexing questions."

"For sure, Janet, for sure," Joannie replied. "Would you like a soda? Hersh put some in my small refrigerator. I'll have a Coke, now that my sugar count doesn't matter anymore. How about you?"

"Sure, I'll join you. All this talking has made me thirsty, too."

As I poured Cokes over ice and handed the glass to Joan, I thought about how Coke had always been her drink of choice. Diabetes had limited that joy from her life as well. Now it no longer mattered. "That tastes so wonderful," Joan said, as she swallowed her first sip. "I may have to have a few more before the day is over." A few more, before the day is over, ricocheted off the walls of my heart.

We continued to explore memories triggered by pictures of our father's parents standing next to his Aunt Mame, his sister Betty and cousins Mike and Pat, all smiling and waving in front of our grandparents' suburban Philadelphia home. Joan and I talked about how the loss of our father had been compounded by the loss of our entire Irish lineage. Joan spoke about trying to keep in contact with Dad's family through letters. In my case, contact with the Irish lineage that lived in my soul was lost when I was twelve years old. I have always struggled with reconciling the softly sensitive Irish heart with the more pragmatically demonstrative Germanic influences of my mother and my German grandparents.

I told Joan about asking Mother if she ever wondered if their marriage would have survived the tensions inherent in their Irish-German heritage. "I expected Mother to think the question outrageous. Instead, she calmly replied that she had often asked herself the same question after Dad's death. She thought Dad was having an affair, but then concluded that his indifference towards her was most likely the brain tumor stealing him away. She mentioned how much she enjoyed going to the racetrack with him, but made clear it was also a means of controlling his gambling habit. Little did she realize that after he was gone, she would be forced by his bookies to pay off his gambling debts. Makes me shudder, Joan, to think those bookies could have been just taking advantage of a traumatized widow."

I went on, "Mother made clear how much she loved Dad's Irish 'eat-drink-and-be-merry' persona which tended to soften her more pragmatic and restrictive Germanic tendencies. I often remember him telling Mother to enjoy today since tomorrow would take care of itself. Ironic. As it turned out, her Germanic instincts ended up having to compensate for his Irish joie de vivre. Mother explained that I could choose to look at my Irish-German lineage as conflicted and difficult, or I could see it as a blessing. She told me to think of my Irish eat-drink-and-be-merry tendencies as offsetting the more severely restrictive Germanic values, and vice versa. Mother had said, 'As I have watched my children mature, I have always thought I could see the humane, fun-loving Irish side of your father and the strong and disciplined Germanic overtones of my personality as offsetting strengths. I have always considered the Irish-German lineage a blessing.'"

Joannie reflected for a moment. "Interesting, Janet," she replied. "You and I must have Irish hearts because both you and I struggled with Mother's determined and often invasive personality. Don't get me wrong; I loved her, but I always felt defensive, protective of those I loved when I was around her. She felt no remorse when she invaded one's space. Even as a small child, I found Mother very difficult to please. Whenever I expressed myself she always felt she needed to correct who I was, what I felt, what I wanted to wear. As an adult, I felt forced to keep some reasonable distance between us. I always had the feeling that she could smother my soul if given a chance. I've often wondered if Dad felt smothered as well."

Sighing deeply and looking past me towards the window, Joan reflected, "Ever since Dad died, Janet, I've struggled with a sense of guilt about wishing that Mother, and not Dad, had died. Isn't that an awful thought to have carried in your heart for so many years?"

"Don't feel guilty, Joan. I don't think you should feel guilty about wishing Dad had lived instead of Mother. Dad always had a way of confirming who people were, and Mother always wanted to rearrange everyone she met to suit her image of who she needed them to be. Allowing others to just be who they are is a challenge for most of us. Mother was particularly challenged in that regard."

Continuing, I asked her, "Do you remember the day Mother persuaded Dad to take you shopping for a prom gown by telling him 'whenever Joan and I shop together, all we do is argue because I want her to buy smart, tailored clothes, and she always wants fussy ribbons and bows? You take her, Jack, she will listen to you.' Do you remember what happened when you came home from your shopping trip with Dad?"

"Of course, I do," Joan replied. "When Mother asked Dad to take me shopping, I was so happy. I knew he and I would have a wonderful day together. When we came home and I got the yellow tulle gown out of the box, Mother turned to him and exclaimed, 'How in the world could you have allowed her to buy that gown? I thought we had agreed that you would guide her choices.'"

"To this day," Joan whispered with a smile, "I carry Dad's reply in my heart. I can still hear him saying, 'Martel, Joan feels like a beautiful princess in this gown. Isn't that all that really matters?'"

"Thanks, Janet, for reminding me of the context of my wish that Mother—not Dad—had died. It lessens some of the guilt. Right now, under my circumstances, that brings me great relief."

"Oh my, Joannie, no guilt necessary. Your reaction to Dad's loss was perfectly logical."

"Do you remember how hard you struggled to free yourself from Mother's parental dominance when you were a teenager, Janet? I do. I won my battle when I married Hersh and left home. But you lost your battle. I always worried that you would never be able to free yourself."

"I certainly do remember our battles," I told her, "but the intensity of those battles subsided somewhat when I went away to prep school. They re-intensified when I moved back to Pennsylvania as a married woman with children. It was only the last few years of Mother's life that I found extremely difficult, but I always tried to keep in mind the intensity of her emotional and physical needs as she aged. I do agree, Joan, the intensity of her own needs often blinded her to the damage she could inflict on the spirits of her children. I suspect that was exactly what she was saying in her third letter."

"Oh, I think that's right, Janet."

A nurse popped her head in the room to ask if Joan needed pain medication. Joan said no, she was doing all right. "But, thank you for checking," she said with a soft smile as the nurse shut the door.

"You know, Joannie, I have spent a good bit of time struggling to understand why I am so driven by the need to save rabbits, to minimize life's struggles for those around me. Do you remember the day I carried the bloody rabbit that Dad and John had shot back to Clyde's house so Mother could help me save it? At seven years of age, I was traumatized by the violent death of that small bunny and felt compelled to try to save it. Obviously we could not.

There it was, the connection: "When Dad suffered and died, and neither God nor the doctors saved him, I think I unconsciously determined that 'saving rabbits,' doing whatever I could do to minimize suffering for those I loved, was to be my life's work. What I didn't realize then, but am now beginning to understand, is that saving rabbits not only requires the saver to be exhaustively vigilant about the needs of others, but may ultimately doom the rabbits she is trying to save. I have come to understand that some rabbits don't want to be saved, some rabbits don't yet recognize they need saving, some rabbits' definitions of being saved will dramatically differ from my own. And, ultimately, rabbits grow strong by figuring out how to save themselves. And that challenge can only be met by the rabbit first figuring out who it really is."

"Since Mother's death, I have felt free to explore who I really am as opposed to who Mother, Phil, my kids and the rest of the world needed me to be—kind of a scary process, but exhilarating at the same time. During this self-imposed internal odyssey, I have come to realize that some of my greatest fears are those of disapproval and failure—the disapproval which pressures me to define myself as others need me to be and the fear of failure which forces me to strive for perfection while simultaneously feeling unable to take risks. Those fears have sapped my self-confidence and increased my need to define myself by what others need.

"I have come to understand that if you are always engaged in pleasing others, you end up never pleasing yourself. I have just recently realized, Joannie, that the real long-term psychological consequence of losing Dad is the loss of a large part of ourselves. After all, it was our job to keep Mother safe, to please her, to ensure her love and support. A really complicated state of affairs, don't you think?"

Joan replied, "I think all of us had to find ways to adapt ourselves to live with Mother's need to be in control. As a boy, John's relationship was defined differently, and as the oldest, I was able to leave home several years after Dad's death, I don't think I was as vulnerable as you and Joyce. You and Joyce had to please."

"I call it adaptive survival, Joannie. When we lost Dad, leaving Mother as our sole source of love and support, we lived in fear that something would happen to her. So in order to take care of her emotional needs, we compromised our own. I know I learned early on to develop antennae that were supersensitive to others' body language and facial expressions, understanding that if others were OK, I was going to be OK."

Joan remained silent for a few minutes, and then said, "I certainly remember all of us overhearing the adult discussions after Dad's death about putting us in foster care because Mother would not be able to survive alone with four children. I certainly remember Della telling us that she did not expect Mother to live very long because she was under far too much stress and how she cautioned us that it was our job to take good care of Mother by being on our best behavior."

"Yes," I replied. " I remember asking myself if part of the reason Dad died was that I had not always been on my best behavior. The message had been dramatically delivered, your mother survives, you survive. Wow, Joannie, this certainly helps me to understand some of my own idiosyncrasies and fears. Maybe that's part of the reason I felt such relief after Mother's passing. I think I instinctively understood that my need to be who Mother needed me to be was over. I was free to turn inward to find me, to find my authentic voice."

Joan nodded and turned her eyes toward the windows in deep reflection. "Mother's death gave you permission to find your authentic voice, Janet. Her death gave me permission to withdraw from dialysis. At her funeral I sobbed, listening to the letters that she left for us, but I also wept because I felt so relieved that my struggle to spare her the death of a child was over."

Feeling a surge of emotions that I feared I could not control, I quickly turned our discussion back to the collage. "Joannie, on another subject, let me ask you about what you know about Mother's relationship with Dad's parents. The collage pictures that show the happy times we spent with our grandparents dramatically conflict with what Mother shared with us after Dad's death. Do you remember Mother's stories about how cruelly Dad's parents treated him? I remember one story she told about a Christmas visit to Dad's parents' home when Aunt Betty received many gifts and Dad's father threw him half a pack of razor blades. Wow, I was stunned by the cruelty towards Daddy!"

"I also remember Mother telling stories about their total lack of support when Dad was in the hospital for tests and the brain surgery. Mother spoke of staying at their house but having to take a cab back and forth to the hospital, about how they never came to visit while he was hospitalized and how she had to travel home on the train by herself to tell us about Dad's diagnosis following the surgery. She alluded to a 'nasty go-round' while she was staying with them, but never filled in any of the particulars."

"If my memory serves me right, Dad's parents and his Aunt Mame came for frequent visits while we were growing up, always seemed to have a good time, always brought beautiful presents for all of us and attended Dad's funeral following the 'nasty go-round' that occurred while he was hospitalized. Mother never elaborated, so I never really understood what happened. I have never been able to reconcile my memories with what Mother told us about their uncaring attitudes. Did you ever figure out what happened that caused the split?" I asked.

"As the first-born grandchild," Joan explained "I tried to stay in touch with the Bradys because I had many fond memories of time spent with them as a child and a young adolescent. I used to go to visit with them over the summer and felt they cared deeply about me. I wrote to them frequently after Dad's death, then somewhat less frequently as time went on. Daddy Jim died, followed by Mezzie, and then eventually Aunt Mame. They never spoke about the reasons for losing touch, and I never asked. Following our grandparents' deaths I stayed in touch with Aunt Betty and even tried to stay in touch with cousins Pat and Mike after Aunt Betty's death. Eventually, over the years, I lost touch with Pat and Mike as well. Sad, isn't it?"

I shared my theory with Joan that maybe Dad's parents resented Mother for encouraging Dad to leave the Philadelphia dental practice that he and his dad shared so they could move closer to her parents in Camp Hill. "I have just always assumed that they were bitter towards Mother for totally rearranging the plans they had for their son's future. I remember Mother saying that Dad's parents never offered to help her after his death because they said, 'she was strong and independent and could manage on her own.' They seemed to be sure she would be fine. Sounds like some kind of quiet revenge to me. Whatever broke loose between Mother and our grandparents had to be traumatic. Mother must have made the conscious decision to give up all contact with them. That decision painfully compounded the loss of Dad, and our Irish lineage vanished. Let's face it, Mother was our total lifeline."

Joannie looked tired, so I asked if she would like to stop for the day. She insisted that we should talk about a couple more collage pictures before stopping.

I wanted to leave her with happy thoughts to think about through the night, so I chose pictures from our childhood and teen years that captured memories before Dad's illness became known. One photo showed Joan standing in front of a blossoming-pale-pink peony garden, hands tucked into her knee-high-rolled up jeans, and sporting a short-sleeved plaid summer shirt and sneakers with no socks. Both her smile and her deep bobbed-shiny-black hair reflected sunlight. "Geez, Joan, you actually have sneakers on. I don't think I can remember a dozen times during the summer when you wore shoes."

Joannie laughed, "Ironic isn't it that I could never stand to wear shoes on my feet, and now if I still had my feet I would be more than happy to wear shoes."

I grimaced at her comment.

I described another picture of Joan, at four years of age, dressed in a pastel-spring dress and matching sweater with her hands clasped together in front of her. John is about two-and-a-half, in white trousers and striped sweater, and Mother in a skirt, sweater and blouse is smiling and holding me in her arms. We are standing next to Joan. "I think because of our ages and the white picket fence in the background, it had to be the small house on 23rd Street where you, John and I were all born and where Dad had opened his first dental office. Remember the beautiful weeping willow tree in the backyard? It's in the picture."

Joannie's face softened and a warm smile crossed her face. "I sure do," she replied. "I used to play house with my dolls under its branches."

We laughed about how Mother always told us stories of having three young children and only three very small bedrooms. Joan had her bedroom, John and I shared cribs in another bedroom, and Mother and Dad had their bedroom. Joan and I recalled numerous stories that Mother used to tell us about the challenges she faced trying to ride herd on her very active kids, while Dad worked with patients in the office connected to the house.

I recalled Mother's story about the day John climbed out of his crib, climbed into mine and woke me up from my nap by stealing my bottle. Responding to the sounds of screaming, Mother arrived to remove us both from my crib with instructions to play nicely together on the floor with our toys. She said she had only been downstairs for a short time when she heard the sound of running water. As she dashed from the kitchen, she saw water running down the stairs. Frantically, she arrived upstairs to find the bathroom door locked, with water pouring under the door and John giggling with glee, saying, "Throw something in the water, Janet; throw something in the water."

Mother calmly tried to instruct John how to unlock the bathroom door, but each time he tried he failed. Realizing that she was not going to get John to unlock the door, she ran across the street to borrow a ladder from a neighbor. Climbing to the second floor, praying that the window was not locked, Mother said she visualized one or both of us floating face-down in the bathtub. She shimmied the window open, climbed inside to discover that John and I had been floating anything we could get our hands on in the bathtub.

Laughing, Joan said, "Yes, I clearly remember that story. I think Mother told it a thousand times while we were growing up. How could any of us forget?"

"Janet, do you remember the other 23rd Street story, about the day Mother tied John to the backyard porch with a rope? He must have been about three. She said she felt so bad about having to do it that she decided she would give him enough rope so he could play, but not enough rope to climb the fence. Satisfied that she had confined him safely, she went back inside to prepare dinner. Minutes later someone knocked at the front door, and when she went to answer it, she found John with a big satisfied smile on his face. He had scaled the fence, trotted down the sidewalk, climbed onto the front porch and knocked at the door, all the while still being tied to the back porch. Mother always cracked up laughing when she told that story."

"Lord, yes, Joan. She told that story a million times as well."

Noticing that Joan looked exhausted, I asked her if she would like to lie down to rest before dinner. "I will be back early tomorrow and we can continue reminiscing about all the crazy folks on the family collage."

"No," Joan said, "I don't want to go to bed. I'll just rest here on the chair and wait for Hersh to come for dinner. See you tomorrow, Janet. I'll be looking forward to talking some more about the collage. Isn't it amazing that almost all those loved ones we have been talking about are gone? Only you, John, Joyce, and I remain. Guess there will be a crowd to greet me when I get there," she laughed.

"Does that thought comfort you, Joan?

"Very much so," she replied.

I thought about the stress she must be feeling as she mentally and emotionally prepared to die. She had to be asking herself if death would come today, this hour, this very moment. When? How? How much pain would she feel? She had to be emotionally exhausted. Suddenly, I felt the full extent of my own emotional exhaustion. As I collected my purse and car keys for the trip home, my legs felt like they would not sustain me. "See you tomorrow, sweet sister. It has been a wonderful day."

"It sure has," she softly replied. "These treasured reminiscences will remain in my heart forever."

Walking to the car, I thought about her word "forever" and wondered what that really meant.

Time . . . so little time left.

As I began the drive home, I wept so hard I had to pull over to the side of the road. It felt like shattered pieces of my soul were dropping into a deep black hole. I felt so constrained about what I could talk with Joan about . . . so many questions I wanted to ask. Did she have any regrets about her decision to remove herself from dialysis? Was she scared of dying? What was she currently feeling inside her body? Did she believe she would be with Mother and Dad again? I wanted to make her promise that if there was something beyond life as we know it, she would find a way to let me know. But I never asked, fearing that my questions would cause her anguish.

When I pulled into my driveway at home, I saw the golden-red sun setting. *My God, this could be her last sunset. I may only have tomorrow to make sure she knows how much she has meant in my life. I just don't understand why this gentle angel has to suffer so, has to die.* "Help me, someone, to stop what is happening. I cannot do this," I cried aloud. I heard only silence.

CHAPTER TWENTY-FIVE

HOW DO I SAY GOOD-BYE?

U woke up very early the next day, determined to spend as much time with Joan as I could. As I hurriedly dressed, my heart felt such dread that it throbbed erratically, and I wondered if it would be able to sustain me through the day.

I called Joyce and told her to come if she wanted to say a final good-bye to Joan. "I don't think she will be here tomorrow, Joyce. She is getting a lot weaker. Come as soon as you can." Joyce said she would come mid-day. I didn't bother to call John since I had already called to tell him that it would mean the world to Joan if he could stop by. I knew by the tone of his reply that he couldn't bring himself to visit, but when I arrived back at Joan's apartment her face was aglow as she said, "You'll never guess who called me! John! It was so wonderful to hear his voice. I am so grateful that he called." My heart felt joy and gratitude that she had heard our brother's voice and felt his concern.

Joan's daughter, Martel, had slept on the living room couch through the night. Joan was already dressed and in her chair. Martel told me that, on the advice of the retirement home staff, her dad had contacted hospice and that they would be sending someone to talk with the family sometime early afternoon. Martel looked exhausted, so I suggested she go home to shower and rest, assuring her that I would stay with her mother until she returned. She thanked me and left.

Joan's face was drawn and pale, a mirror of her growing discomfort. When I asked if there were anything I could do to make her more comfortable, she said, "My lower back is throbbing, and no matter which way I sit, it doesn't seem to help. But let's not worry about that now, let's just talk about the collage."

"If you lean forward, Joan, and let me massage your back near your kidneys maybe that will give you some relief. I will ask the nurse on duty about getting you some pain medication."

As I rubbed her back, I thought about how it was the first time I had physically touched my sister since we were very young children. With my own children, I had to learn to hug and learn to feel comfortable saying "I love you" out loud. I found demonstrative love so gratifying to my soul that I had to be sensitive to the fact that others might prefer a more subdued expression of caring.

"That feels wonderful, Janet. It has provided me with a bit of relief. Thank you so much. Don't spend time searching for the nurse, she will stop by soon, I'm sure. I want to have time to talk further about the collage before the hospice folks get here," she urged.

"OK," I replied, "but if the nurse does not come soon, I'm going to find her. I don't want you to suffer needlessly."

I studied the collage and made a mental note to select pictures of Mother and Dad that Joan would be able to hold onto as she slipped into unconsciousness, vivid pictures to reassure her they would be waiting for her at the end of her journey.

I described Dad at 23rd Street, dressed in pants and a tie with his white dress shirt sleeves rolled up, holding Joan when she was an infant, and another of Mother in a short-sleeved two-piece summer dress holding baby Joan. I described the look of love and joy on both their faces. I told her of baby Joannie, in another picture, lying on her tummy naked, kicking her legs in the air on a blanket in the sunny backyard near the weeping willow tree.

There was a gentle knock as the door opened. The nurse poked her head in and asked if we needed anything. "Joan is having a good bit of discomfort. Can you provide some relief?"

"Of course; I have some medication with me that will help. I want you to know, Joan, that whenever you need further medication, just let me know. My job is to keep you as comfortable as possible."

As the nurse gave Joan a shot, Joan smiled sweetly and thanked her. "It is comforting to know you are there," Joan said. The nurse left, saying she would check back in a while to make sure Joan's pain was controlled.

"OK, Janet, let's not waste anymore time. Let's get back to our collage discussions."

"I have thought a lot about the hardships Mother faced growing up. How joyous she felt when she met Dad and had her four children. At last she must have felt her life had been respectably fulfilled and her status restored, loneliness banished forever. Then, after only seventeen years of marriage, her prince was ripped from her life. Dad was 47; Mother was only 40 years of age. Left with four children to raise, no money and shattered dreams, her steel will, determination and strength she built growing up were indeed sorely needed.

"Even though, like you, I had conflicts with Mother over some of her more hurtful invasions into my life, I always tried to put them into the context of her life. Sometimes I was more successful than others," I laughed. "Truly, her children were her world, so when we married and had families of our own, Mother perceived our marriages as threats to her well-being. Like the medieval knights of old, she crossed the moat in full-body armor, attacked whatever she perceived as a threatening foe, and then quickly retreated behind her protective fortress walls. Mother's protective fortress walls did, indeed, keep out her enemies. Tragically they also prevented loved ones from crossing the moat bearing gifts of healing, love and peace."

"Good heavens, yes," Joan exclaimed. "I always loved her dearly, but she could be so invasive, so meddling, so self-focused at times. I agree, her life was difficult, and I, too, tried to understand, but I had to create distance between us. Often her love hurt a lot, created conflicts in relationships that were important to me, and complicated my marriage. Isn't it amazing, Janet, that after someone dies, we often get to know them better than we did in life?"

"Well, Joannie, I think when a parent dies, a part of us is freed to gain perspectives and insights about them, as well as ourselves and to accept that each of us carries darkness and light within our beings. We give up our youthful idealized need to see perfection in those we love and learn to accept that all adult relationships have conditional moments. We make peace with the darker sides of loved ones' personalities by putting their specific actions into the broader context of their lives."

"I believe that our relatively idyllic childhood, full of love and nurturing, in conjunction with our painful losses, built strength into our beings. I think we have, each in our own way, used that strength to discover the Light of our inner cores. When life challenges me with more than I can bear, I turn there for hope and courage. I know, Joannie, that your pocket of divinity is very large. All through your life you have loved and nourished those around you. Your quiet courageous soul has sustained me throughout these many years. You have lived in the light, Joannie. Having you as my sister and my friend has strengthened my light and provided me with great joy."

"Thank you, Janet. It brings me great peace to hear you say that I have succeeded as your sister and friend. I hope I have been a good mother, spouse, and daughter as well."

"Joannie, when I look at the collage pictures of you as an infant, I see the joy on Mother's and Dad's faces. When I see their prideful expressions as they look at you as a beautiful adolescent, I know how deeply they loved you and how proud they were of who you were becoming."

There was another soft knock at the door. Joyce arrived. She seated herself and anxiously asked Joan how she was feeling.

"I'm doing OK, all things considered. They have given me some medication to take the edge off the pain. A hospice worker will be stopping in to talk with us soon. Hersh and Martel will be joining us for that discussion, so let's not waste any more time talking about me. Janet and I were just reminiscing about Mother and Dad."

We sat together, three sisters laughing and sharing old memories. Most particularly, we shared the sweet memories of Barleycroft. We reminisced about the gala parties with candy-striped tents, the basement refrigerator with a tap for beer and a tap for Coke, swimming in the lake and lying on the sandy beach while Black Angus steers and thoroughbred horses grazed nearby, the magnificent Christmases with all five fireplaces ablaze, country club staff with tall white hats serving bubbling soup from the kitchen's large copper cauldrons, freshly-cut Christmas trees sparkling with white lights, bundles of meadow greens and pine cones adorning mantels, staircases, large antique crocks, and all the deep window sills. The three of us agreed that Barleycroft was the essence of family and beautiful memories for us and our children, and even many of our friends.

As I sat listening to the laughter wrapped around beautiful moments, I could not help but think about how soon it would be two, not three, sisters sharing laughter and memories. *Soon, I will be older than Joan is now. I will become the oldest sister. My God, how absolutely bizarre. How can this be happening?* I felt anguished by the idea that soon I would never see Joan again . . . never again meet her at Bender's for lunch . . . never again sit in her family room talking about the latest great books we had read . . . never walk with her through the woods to the lake near her cabin . . . never be able to seek her quiet counsel when I needed reassurance and nurturance.

Hersh, Martel and the hospice worker arrived simultaneously. I stood silently frozen in the moment, as my heart raced and pounded in anticipation. The hospice worker quietly sat down next to Joan and began to walk her through the procedures that they would follow. She explained that she would work with Joan's doctor to administer whatever pain medications she would need, address any questions or concerns that Joan or the family had, and be there whenever Joan or any of the family needed her. Joan asked for some additional medication for her kidney pain.

The decision was made to place a hospital bed in Joan's room next to her white, rose bud enhanced queen-sized bed. When the hospice worker left, I felt great relief to know that she was on call at any time night or day to assist with Joan's pain. Her calm, reassuring demeanor provided a modicum of peace. I thought, Bless you and your fellow volunteers for what you do.

Martel said she was going to leave for a short while to meet her brothers Hershey and Brady and her sister-in-law Sue at the house, so they could all return together to spend the evening with Joan. Hersh, Joyce and I waited for the hospital bed to be set up. It was clear that the morphine and Joan's kidney failure were taking an enormous physical toll. Joan indicated that she was really tired and wanted to go to bed to rest. It was going to take some time for the hospital bed to arrive, so the nurses decided to move Joan into her regular bed. As they did so, Joan cried out in pain. Settling herself into a curled fetal position, she quietly thanked them for their help. I marveled at the beauty of her heart.

Sometime later the hospital bed arrived. Joyce and I could not bear to hear Joan cry out again in pain as they moved her, so we walked the halls while they resettled her. I told Joyce that I thought Joan's children should have time alone with her, so I planned to go home and return early in the morning. Joyce agreed and said she too would return home.

Hersh had settled himself in the living room to watch the basketball game and wait for their kids to arrive. Joyce and I went into say good-bye to Joan. She never opened her eyes. As we left the bedroom, my eyes burned with tears and my lower back throbbed with pent-up emotion. I turned my head and over my shoulder whispered, "Goodbye, Joannie. I love you always and forever."

After promising to call Joyce tomorrow, I sat in my car in the parking lot for I don't know how long. Bizarre thoughts ran through my mind. I looked at the building and worried about how Joan's soul would pass through the roof. I thought about a party at my brother's when she looked so beautiful in a black-and-silver dress and thought about how much I would love to have that dress to keep always. I thought about the Hallmark plaque that Joan had given me some years ago as we were having lunch.

I had laughed and asked what the occasion was. She said, "No occasion, I saw it and I wanted to give it to you." I hung the plaque next to my dressing room table where I could see it as I began each day, right under a picture of Joannie at age eight with ribbon-tied pigtails, standing with one hand on

John's shoulder and one hand on mine. I thought about how her hand had always remained gently on my shoulder no matter how many years passed, no matter the distance between us. The exact Hallmark verse on the plaque was also printed in a card she sent me for my birthday one year later. I repeated the words out loud, hoping, as she lay dying she could somehow hear me.

MY SISTER

She knows just where I dream to go,
Remembers where I've been,
Accepts me just the way I am, and treats me
Like a friend—
She's someone who is there for me
No matter what or when,
And every time I'm with her,
It's like coming home again.

Through a veil of tears, I shouted, "I love you, Joannie. God Speed, sweet sister. Say hi to Mother and Dad for me."

Phil was waiting for me when I arrived home. I collapsed onto the couch, telling him that I did not know if Joan would live through the night. I had begun to share some of the day with him when Hersh called to say that Joan had died. Immediately, I felt a great surge of regret that I had not remained with her. Phil wrapped his arms around me as I hung up the phone, sobbing. He patted me reassuringly through the night as I struggled to reconcile myself to her death.

Life will never be the same again.

Christmas and New Year celebrations will be tempered by the sorrowful reminder of January 4th, 2000, the day Joannie died. In years past I would always say to Phil, "Joan's Christmas card is first again, it must be Christmas!" "Not this year," I sobbed into my pillow. "Not this year nor any other year, forever."

Joan was scheduled to be buried on a Friday. The night before the funeral, I wanted to walk the two blocks from my house to the funeral home to see her one more time. My daughter Susan called and told the funeral home that I wished to come and spend some time alone with Joan. How ironic, I thought, that she was being buried from a funeral home in the city, since she had always been fearful about coming into the city. When the time arrived for me to go, I could not. The thought of seeing her lying in a casket tore my heart apart. In some bizarre way, I felt like I was letting her down by not going for one more good-bye. I felt so conflicted. Then I remembered the sister's plaque and her telling me how I had always been there for her. I knew Joan would understand why I had not come. She died with my love in her heart, that's all that matters now, I thought.

Somehow the mind and body shroud themselves in a kind of foggy gauze, allowing the soul to survive traumatic events. As I sat next to my brother John at the church memorial service, he said, "I never really knew Joan."

I patted his knee and whispered, "What a shame, John. She was truly a wonderful person and a dear friend. She spoke of you often. I know she loved you very much." Following the memorial service, Joan was buried in the cemetery behind the church. I had brought one peach rose which I placed on top of her casket. After the burial as everyone began to walk towards the church for brunch, I looked at Phil and through my tears said, "I cannot do this. I cannot leave her, not yet. I have to go back to be with Joan."

The men preparing to lower her casket were unnerved by our return and asked if they should wait to finish their task. "No," I replied, "I just want to be with my sister as you lower her casket." I watched the peach rose disappear into the earth and felt such horror that my beautiful sister would be trapped alone in the darkness under the earth. I wanted to scream, Stop, I need to figure out a way to keep her with me. I sat in silence as my heart began to bleed. I felt like I was suffocating. When the workers picked up their shovels, I took the first handful of dirt and sprinkled it over her coffin. "I love you, Joannie, I love you," I whispered, and Phil and I walked towards the church.

Phil stayed by my side at the memorial reception at the church, knowing that I did not want to be there. One of Joan's close friends, who never went to visit with her while she was in the retirement home, approached me and I looked the other way. I said to another friend loudly how much it had meant to Joan that she had come to visit her on a regular basis with news of friends and town activities. I thought, I let her know, Joan, how deeply she hurt you. When you desperately needed her friendship most, she walked away and she needn't pretend it was otherwise now that you're gone.

I felt compelled to visit Joan's gravesite after dark for many months, so I could lay on the ground, with my hands pressed against the cold earth over her grave, and wail out the pain that threatened to consume me. Sobbing with disbelief, I crawled on my hands and knees to stroke the letters of her name, Joan Brady Groff, carved into the unforgiving cold gray stone of her headstone.

I felt the cold winter nights, starkly barren trees, and whistling wind somehow connected me more intimately with my sister who lay in such darkness. I hoped that sitting and kneeling and pounding on the earth above her in the darkness would connect us, help her to know that I was there and to feel me. I mentally agonized to accept the notion that my beautiful sister was really in a box underground. It just didn't seem possible to me. I even fantasized about digging her up and taking her home with me so she would never be alone.

I wrote the words from the sister's plaque she had given me, sealed it in an envelope and left it at her gravesite as my gift back to her. One night, as I turned my back to her grave and looked up to a sky filled with brilliant stars, I knew the intensity of the loss would diminish in time, but that my world would never be the same.

Time passed, the wailing turned to tears and the tears to a stoic acceptance of my loss. After many months, I came to accept that her essence had flown home on angel's wings. My beloved sister was free, and I was left with the precious memories of our last days together. In the late spring of 2004, I visited her gravesite to say, "Joannie, I have decided to go up to our Cape Cod house for the summer to try to heal the throbbing open wounds left by your death and Mother's. I will treasure all the sweet memories I have of our time together on this earth. I feel so blessed to have had you as my sister. Good-bye for now, sweet angel. I love you dearly, always will. I will come to talk with you when I return in the fall."

"Full to bursting.
The sea accepts, widens our reception.
We are overflowing and the sea contains us.
And then when we are stretched,
when we are broadened,
opened up to a new life,
the sea gives us back to ourselves."

Susan St. John Rheault
CAPE COD MAGAZINE, OCT. 2004

" . . . The peninsula-Cape Cod is essentially
a gigantic sandbox atop underground
deposits of freshwater held in place by the
hydrodynamics of the Atlantic, like hands in
prayer, from the fingertips at Provincetown
to the wrists at the Cape Cod canal."

Cape Cod Magazine
JUNE 2004

CHAPTER TWENTY-SIX

SANCTUARY

I awakened early to the warmth of the Cape Cod sun kissing my face. I lay, snuggled in my bed, thinking about the intensity of last evening's memories of Joan's illness and death. I felt a stirring of peace. Joannie, you were right, it is time for me to move on. Sweet memories of you will always remain in my heart, but it is time to fully re-embrace life. Love you.

Today I was off to Wellfleet to walk one of the most magnificent nature trails on the Cape at the Audubon Bird Sanctuary. It would help my spirit to move on. I showered, jumped into a pair of white shorts and brightly colored top then slipped into my favorite walking sneakers. I slathered myself with sunscreen, stashed bug repellent, water, a bottle of wine and a plastic wine glass in my backpack, donned my sunglasses and grabbed a Portuguese muffin with cream cheese for breakfast on my way out the door.

On the drive to Wellfleet, I felt enormously grateful for this special slice of time to be alone with myself, free to create and plan each day around my own internal rhythms and to have the luxury of time and silence to allow the beauty of this place to penetrate my soul without any distractions. My summer alone was fast drawing to an end. I felt confident that the arduous process of exorcising many demons had taught me introspective skills as well as a deeper understanding of life's purposes that would remain my spiritual template after I left this sacred place. The summer had begun with overwhelming sorrow mixed with an angry confusion; it was ending with transformative feelings of enlightenment, forgiveness, and rebirth.

After a half-hour drive in hectic and heavy traffic, I turned off the main road into the quiet reflective space of the sanctuary. I found exactly that . . . sanctuary, a place of reflective isolation for humans as well as many other creatures.

The scent of the ocean's briny essence mixed with the pungent smell of decomposing leaves on the forest floor reached my nose as I opened the car window and sunroof. My heart fluttered in anticipation of immersing myself in this magnificently beautiful place.

Circling the Audubon visitors' center and striking off down the path, I noticed that the trees had begun to dress themselves in *soft hues of rose* in preparation for winter. Descending the sandy path, with the air hinting at the approach of fall's cool, crisp, crystalline days, I began to anticipate my return to family and friends. A rabbit scampered across my path, reminding me of all the "saving" left to do. Suddenly, the forested area gave way to a small wooden bridge with a salt water pond on one side and a panoramic view of a salt marsh on the other, a view that hinted of even more magnificent vistas to come.

As I paused by the salt pond to watch painted turtles sunning themselves on the exposed tops of submerged rocks, my peripheral vision caught a flash of blue. I froze in perfect stillness. There, on top of a cat-o-nine tail, proudly sat a vibrantly-blue male Kingfisher. I whispered to him of my joy at making his acquaintance and how pleased I would be to add him to my bird sightings list when I returned to the Cape house. He turned his magnificent crested head in my direction, as if acknowledging my appreciation and with a twinkle in his eye, flew heavenward.

I resumed my stroll and ascended through woods of scrub pines and oaks, thinking about the marvelous foresight of those who had battled to prevent the destruction of this wonderful place. I thanked my unknown benefactors for protecting this portion of the Cape's forest and pristine beaches from development and preserving for all time this most beautiful Cape treasure.

Bayberry, scrub pines and oaks, with the distant hint of brine carried on the wind cradled my senses as I climbed a small wooden staircase to a bird watching platform. My eyes feasted on a translucent azure sky, bands of salt marsh grasses of emerald green and gold, traversed by sparkling iridescent navy-blue rivulets. Herons gracefully stalking through the rivulets, pausing in statuary-like stillness, listening, then moving ever so slightly until their long slender bills were well-positioned over their unsuspecting prey, and striking with lightning speed. Humans, unsuspecting and vulnerable, are struck with no warning as well. Just part of the circle of life.

Sandy paths led in every direction, some directly to a

tranquilly unpopulated stretch of beach, others to a hilly island in the middle of the marsh; others still doubled back to the visitors' center through additional forest trails. *Which path should I follow? Do all paths lead to the same destination? If I choose one path over another, will I regret that I did not choose the other?* I decided to follow the path through the hilly island, where trees obscured both its direction and its steepness. More challenging, but that would make my arrival at my destination even more rewarding, I thought.

As I entered the island's woods, the shaded silence wrapped its arms around me. I paused a while on a bench overlooking the marsh. Robert Frost's poetic encouragement to blaze our own unique path, "Two roads diverged in a wood, and I, I took the one less traveled by, and that has made all the difference," filled my mind. We do indeed have to make many tough choices on this road of life. Part of the answer, I think, is making peace with the choices you have made, leaving any regrets about other paths, not chosen, behind. For, even though we may wish we could travel multiple paths, we cannot. And, since "we may never pass this way again" it is essential for us to fully embrace the path we have chosen, lest our regrets overshadow the profound insights and joy our chosen path offers.

I had just grabbed my binoculars from my backpack and begun to scan the marsh, when an enormous blue-gray shadow suddenly rose from the top of a distant clump of pines. I found myself holding my breath and feeling light headed, as the shadow moving across the marsh towards me evolved into a great blue heron. It's like watching an elephant fly, I thought. With its neck and legs fully extended, its huge wings flapping as if in slow motion, the indescribably large bird soared over me and disappeared.

Unburdened by the summer's many blessings, my soul was preparing itself to risk soaring again. So many insights provided, so many lessons learned . . . lessons about fortitude and courage, about when to cross emotionally self-protective moats to do battle and when to retreat back behind fortified walls . . . lessons about fully embracing the path chosen and about lifting heavy burdens skyward with determination and elegant grace. Oh, that everyone struggling with this difficult journey might have their hearts emboldened by a peaceful sanctuary such as this, I whispered. I will carry the Great Blue Heron's flight in my soul forever, and when I fear flying, I will rekindle the image of his magnificent and courageous flight as a reminder to help me soar.

At the path's highest point, a vista of indescribable beauty came into sight. Miles of uninterrupted white beaches softly embraced by a glasslike violet sea, without any hint of humankind, spoke to me of the creative harmony and power of God, Inner Light, Spirit? I realized the definitive God of my childhood had morphed into the more ambiguous Spirit of my adulthood. Suddenly, I heard inside my head, "See Me, Janet, see Me."

"I have seen you," I whispered in reply. My thoughts immediately shifted to the birth of my grandson, a miracle baby, since my daughter had been told it was most unlikely that she would ever have a child. He was only moments old the first time I looked into his eyes, and instead of looking into the unknowing eyes of an infant, I felt as if I was looking into the eyes of a wise old man. My heart pounded and my eyes filled with tears, as I leaned closer to him, sliding my index finger inside his tiny fist to whisper, "You have been here before, haven't you? I see you." His eyes never wavered from my face, as if he were telling me he had arrived to ease the intensity of my beloved Susan's struggle, to fill her heart with a indescribable joy that would remind her how much the Spirit truly loves her.

Loss of life. Renewal of life. Circle of Life. I felt the power of the Blue Heron's wings lifting my spirit heavenward.

Settling myself onto a sandy knoll overlooking the bay, I thought about how my anger towards the Spirit, carried in my heart ever since the deaths of my father and nephew, had been compounded by my sister's untimely death. My anger had muted and distorted its voice. Not only had I allowed my anger to impair my ability to hear the Spirit's voice, I had arrogantly attempted to instruct The Spirit when and where I needed it to intervene in my life.

As if The Spirit sensed that I might now be able to hear it, I heard a voice inside myself softly say; "I have never left you, Janet. I am always with you. I inhabit all living creatures' sacred cores. Just turn inward and follow the Light. You will find the stillness you seek."

With this epiphany erupting in my mind, I leaped to my feet, shouting, "I have been searching in all the wrong places. The Spirit does not intervene in the day-to-day affairs of this world, but abides within each human's sacred core, a source of strength and comfort. All we need do is turn inward to our innermost core. The Light abides inside me. The Spirit abides inside all living creatures. I have, at last, found Home." I felt like a rainbow filled my heart with glorious hues of love and hope beyond anything I had known.

Slowly descending to the bay, I walked across a small plank boardwalk traversing the high tide marshes teeming with hermit crabs. Busy, busy crabs growing themselves, always on the move from shell house to shell house to accommodate their newfound growth, never mourning the loss of the old, simply embracing the new. Humans should grow themselves the same way, I thought. Throw off the old that feels reassuringly comfortable yet confining and push ahead courageously, growing ourselves towards wholeness, never fearing when the time arrives to throw off the old shell and embrace the new.

Crossing a stretch of sandy white beach, I finally arrived at an uninterrupted beautiful expanse of the sea, still no other human in sight. I set my backpack on the sand, removed my sandals and dashed into the water fully clothed, just as I had done many times as a child. With my face and arms raised skyward, I danced, leaping over the small waves that passed under my feet. Shouting with glee, I dove into deeper water, tucking myself into an underwater somersault, and arose sputtering salt water into the air. I dove again to try my hand at underwater breast stroking, my favorite swimming mode as a youngster. Arising from the water like a baby seal with eyes wide and a smile upon my face, I felt filled with a sense of freedom and joy I had not felt since I was a child. "I have spent most of my life working so hard to become an adult," I shouted, "when all along I should have been fighting to maintain a childlike sense of wonder and spontaneity. I will remember this joyous child's impulsive dip into the sea and follow my child's heart more often," I pledged aloud to myself.

I staggered out of the bay giggling. I may have a child's heart, I laughed, but the old body sure could use a few less years of wear. I dropped to the sand, opened my backpack, poured myself a glass of chardonnay and stretched out on the sand. I was startled awake by the sea lapping at my toes.

As I jumped to my feet, I noticed a full moon emerging in the sky and realized that the sea appeared to be standing still, caught for an instant between the push and the pull of the tides. I too had become almost immobilized by the push and pull of forces in my life, but my summer of ebbing demons and flowing healing insights had grown me enough so that I could now comfortably transition from the God of my childhood to the more ambiguous Spirit of my adulthood . . . to the Light within.

If each of us is given a reservoir of Light, then The Spirit force must be telling us that it is our responsibility to learn how to use that Light to quell the darkness in ourselves and in others, I concluded. I thought about how much more glorious our world could be, if all of us could see and honor the spiritual reservoir in each other. If I harm others, I not only damage their core, but diminish my own. Embracing the notion that there are many acceptable, alternative paths to living life with integrity and goodness could revolutionize the world, I thought, as I slipped into my sandals, grabbed my backpack and headed for the car.

Stopping at The Lost Dog, my favorite local Irish pub, for a glass of wine and a burger, I thought about how wonderful my day had been. My Irish heart never fails to remember my handsome Irish Dad and my beloved Irish stepfather each time I visit this Irish pub. As I ate, I thought about Phil's arrival tomorrow with a certain degree of anxiety about readjusting to another's rhythm once again, while at the same time feeling joy and excitement at a good friend's return

"I would like to propose . . . that the people
we are and the lives that we lead
are determined, for better or worse,
by our loss experiences."

Judith Viorst | NECESSARY LOSSES

CHAPTER TWENTY-SEVEN

RABBIT WARRIOR
RETURNS HOME

U awoke early the following morning to a dark, overcast sky and a soft rain, the weather seemed to be giving me a permission slip to lie in my bed a while longer to reflect upon my summer pilgrimage. I had dispelled many demons, much sorrow, and I had learned skills to guide my future path. I found myself and my Light.

Suddenly, a shaft of sunlight pierced through raindrops, creating a magnificent rainbow that arched across the sky. Every time I see a rainbow now, it will remind me of the joy that filled my heart at the bird sanctuary. I'd like to think that my Light painted this beautiful multicolored bridge across the sky especially for me.

As a child, I wondered if I were to swing myself up onto the arc of colors, shimmy like "Jack and the Beanstalk" to the rainbow's top, then hop off, leaping from cloud to cloud, if I could reach heaven. As an adult, I've been told that rainbows are merely sunlight refracted through raindrops. But, just in case it's possible to leap from cloud to cloud to reach heaven, I know I would not seek a goose who laid golden eggs nor magic harps; I would seek the loved ones I had lost to make sure they were truly home. Or, maybe I could simply choose to believe that the rainbow was The Light's assurance that they indeed were home. Magical thinking, I know, but sometimes magical thinking can lift us onto rainbows.

As I lay pondering rainbows, I also pondered the shard of Light inside myself. *I wonder if my shard dies when I do, or does it return to its creator? Could that be what we call soul? The Spirit is such a mysterious force; I suspect I will have to wait for my answers.*

I spent the rest of the day rushing about in preparation for my upcoming week with Phil, grocery shopping and cooking for candlelight gourmet dinners and setting the table with beautiful pottery, whimsical wine glasses, silver napkin rings, candles and flowers. I placed wine glasses and flowers on the deck's coffee table, knowing that most evenings we would have hor d'oeuvres and drinks on the Cape house deck overlooking the cranberry bog and bay. My hope was that all the special preparations would allow Phil to feel my love and gratitude for him and for his precious understanding and encouragement.

Suddenly, a deep anxiousness crept into my awareness. I had grown into such a different independent self, molting a confining shell, growing, then molting again. *Would I be able to merge gracefully back into my family roles while holding onto parts of myself that I had come to treasure? Would I be able to do this without alienating and confusing those who love me? Be still,* I heard a voice softly whisper inside myself. *This transformative journey of renewal and discovery is not over; you have miles yet to travel. Remember, you carry me with you. Pull on me and I will show you the way.*

While I dressed to go pick up Phil at the Barnstable bus stop, I turned on the television and stepped into the bathroom to put on some lipstick. I heard Bill Moyer's voice introducing philosopher Joseph Campbell. I had always held Bill Moyer's inquisitive intellect in the highest regard, and now I listened captivated as he interviewed Campbell about the power of myths in our lives. Sitting perched on the edge of my chair, and periodically checking my watch, I thought how Campbell's most recent book, *An Open Life*, might prove to be a perfect ending to my summer reading marathon. I had no idea how really perfect it would prove to be.

In the car, I grabbed my cell phone to call Phil. I caught him walking through Boston's Logan Airport to board a Plymouth and Brockton bus to Barnstable. I told him I was stopping at the bookstore to pick up a copy of Campbell's book, but that I was reasonably sure I would make it to the bus stop on time. He chuckled saying, "No problem, if you're not there when the bus gets in, I will wait for you."

I dashed into the bookstore, made my purchase without even looking at it and arrived at the bus stop with plenty of time to spare. I began to scan the book. Campbell believes that "our demons are our own limitations, which shut us off from the realization of the ubiquity of the spirit." Campbell seemed to be confirming my summer efforts to recognize and confront my self-imposed limitations so that I might find the way to my spiritual center. Or, put another way, recognizing my internalized demons makes them powerless to manipulate and disorient, and thus releases me to live a more authentic life.

Campbell also startled me into thinking about my proclivity to save rabbits, as he spoke about American Indian myths, in which the rabbit represents our internal unrecognized creator, an internal energy threatening to break through. Suddenly, I understood my lifetime's instinctive quest to save rabbits. My efforts had been driven by a firm belief that you never, ever, quit on those you love. I believed that love was the singular force that would expel others' demons and let their glory out. Is that what I sense in myself and others, our life forces battling to break free?

I grabbed a tablet out of the center console of my car and wrote. I always thought of others as the rabbits I was struggling to save. What I have realized over these summer months is that one of those rabbits was me.

Amazing! I thought.

For so many years I had struggled to love Phil's vulnerable and damaged rabbit back to wholeness, all the while failing to understand that he, in turn, was lovingly supporting me back to wholeness as well. It was Phil, many years ago, who had made the arrangements for me to attend a writers' conference because he believed I had an untapped talent. Later, he had encouraged me to go back to college to finish my undergraduate degree, and then recognized the intensity of my struggle to right myself after my sister's death. It was Phil who had suggested that I should take a three-month Cape Cod sabbatical, a sabbatical from community and family obligations in order to read, write, and heal myself.

I saw the bus from Boston driving down the exit ramp. I felt nervous excitement. Each time Phil gets on the bus to leave the Cape, I feel anxious, and each time he arrives back

I get butterflies. I could feel the fluttering of butterflies deep within me.

As folks filed off the bus, I thought how lucky I was to have him as my friend. How lucky we had been to make it through the difficult years to this much more soft and nurturing place. Suddenly he appeared at the top of the bus steps with a loving smile on his face, and my eyes filled with tears. He walked to my open car window and kissed me. My heart soared with love for this very special man.

We had a wonderful week—working together to winterize the house, going out to breakfast and dinner, reading, taking walks by the bay and sharing thoughts about the summer. During one of our many walks by the sea, I told Phil I felt somewhat embarrassed to be harboring the notion that I might actually be able to write something worthy of another's consideration, but that using my journal had grown my conviction that I must try to write a book about my summer experience.

"Actually, Phil, for most of my life I have felt there was some unidentified task I was supposed to accomplish. I think I have finally identified that task. Initially, I told myself that I would write just to clarify and capture essential parts of myself, for myself," I shared. "But slowly I have come to believe that my personal insights might add value and perspective to my loved ones' journeys as well, moving my writing efforts from personal journal to family memoir, allowing our daughters to know me in a way that my mother could not allow me to know her. Then, within a quiet corner of my heart, the notion that my writing might touch a broader audience began to grow.

"Maybe my summer has birthed a writer," I giggled.

"Wonderful," he replied, "I always believed that eventually your Irish storytelling abilities would overcome your insecurities, and you would write about your journey. I'll support you any way I can."

When we arrived home from our walk to the beach, Phil poured us each a glass of wine, and we settled down on the deck to watch the sunset. A rabbit emerged from the brush and, using its sharp claws, scratched a small indent-like nest in the sandy soil. I knew that rabbits, always wary of predators, build their nests open in both the front and the back for a quick get-away. I smiled as the gray fuzzy rabbit settled herself into the nest, eyes and ears alert, but seemingly satisfied that she had done all she could to protect herself. She, like us, had come to enjoy the beauty of the setting sun before retiring for the night.

Suddenly, I realized there were no birds at the feeder and none of the normal busy bird calls and rushing about as they settled themselves in the trees for the night. I knew the eerie silence could only mean one thing. I whispered to Phil to get up quietly and see if he could spot whatever threat was nearby. Sure enough, sitting on the branch of a scrub pine was an enormous red-tailed hawk. Its sharp talons were extended around the branch of the tree, and its icy-yellow eyes were singularly focused on the rabbit quietly resting in her nest. She did not appear to see it.

I felt panic. My summer had taught me that nature has its own rhythms and demands and that maybe I should just relax and let nature takes its course. Oh, I agonized, dear little vulnerable rabbit will you be able to make it to the safety of the brush?

I stomped my feet, tore off the deck, and screamed at the hawk, "You big lug. Let that bunny alone." *Oh, my Lord, saving rabbits is truly a part of my life's work. Guess I just have to make peace with that part of myself.*

Phil shouted from the deck, "I knew you could do it, Love. Chalk up another rabbit saved."

As we settled again on the deck to enjoy the last rays of the disappearing sun, we talked about how our summer separation had deepened our appreciation of each other, and provided both of us with the time and space to reflect and grow.

"I think you and I have finally come to understand that there are many doors into each other's hearts, some have been rusted shut by life's more challenging experiences, others have been left slightly ajar in the hopes that the other will take the time to walk lovingly through them," I said to Phil. "Fortunately, when times got really tough, we searched until we found the doors left ajar in each other's hearts. I am thankful that our increased knowledge, garnered over the years, has made doors ajar easier to find."

We promised each other to try not to forget the lessons learned.

As I cooked dinner, I thought about how grateful I was that Phil and I had managed to persevere through so many challenges that had had the potential to destroy our marriage.

Scenes from *On Golden Pond*, a movie that Phil and I had watched together several times, popped into my head: hardships overcome, daughters and fathers reconciled, a husband

and wife's deeply insightful and supportive lifelong commitment. I smiled as I thought about the movie's loons, calling to
one another as they built their baby's nest, raising their young
and teaching them how to fly, flying south at the end of the
summer only to return the following year, committing to one
another for their lifetimes.

It's the only movie Phil and I have watched multiple times.
He tells me I am his Ethel Thayer (Kathryn Hepburn), and I
sometimes refer to him as my "old poop," (Norman Thayer/
Henry Fonda). I frequently think of the scene, where Norman
is having a heart attack, slumped on the front porch of the
cabin and Ethel is frantically trying to call for help and im-
ploring him to, "Hang on. You cannot die, not now." I carry
within my heart the same panic Ethel felt as she considered life
without Norman.

Phil and I see our softly combative relationship reflected
in the roles portrayed by Kathryn Hepburn and Henry Fonda
in *On Golden Pond*. We keep a carved wooden loon on our
bookshelf as a reminder of commitment and fidelity, and often
refer to our beloved Cape Cod Bay as our Golden Pond.

In the morning, we packed the car hurriedly, closed down
the house, and drove to our favorite breakfast spot, The Red
Cottage, to enjoy a gourmet breakfast in a casual and welcom-
ing environment. We ate, mostly in silence, content to be together and when breakfast was over, climbed into the car to
begin the drive home.

As we crossed the Bourne Bridge towards the mainland,
my eyes traveled east over the sparkling blue waters of the canal into the bay and I thought about how transformative my

summer had been. Like my much beloved Cape, I have transformed myself from a mere peninsular extension of family to a much more uniquely me, I whispered inside my head. I have indeed "bourne" another me.

I thought about how homesick and alone I had felt at the beginning of the summer, and how filled with love and companionship I felt now. My spirit had spewed forth an inordinate amount of painful mourning, unburdening my mind so that I could see more clearly. Pilgrims journeyed to Cape Cod seeking freedom and solace from suffering. My summer pilgrimage has set me free and lessened my suffering, as well.

I thought about the creatures that had shown me how to camouflage and retreat when danger threatens, how to live authentically by being true to who I am, how to live integrated into the fabric of the whole, how to anticipate, accept and soar.

I marveled at having randomly selected books from my large canvas bag . . . a randomness that led me where I needed to go. No sequence. No thought of continuity between books, just a voracious appetite to read and reflect. That literary journey had helped to carry me back to myself. Deeply ingrained misconceptions about God had been dispelled, and a new understanding of holiness and its accessibility had taken its place. William Blake's declaration that "all things are holy" resonated in my heart.

All the creatures that had shared their lessons with me-lobsters, horseshoe crabs, hawks, trees, hummingbirds, foxes, whales . . . rabbits and herons-are holy.

The writer's willingness to share honestly her life's journey, to cajole, guide, encourage, provide insights, suggest alternative view-

points, always reminding her readers of the universality of fear,
struggle, joy and loss are holy as well, I thought.

The love and support of my beloved husband, family and
friends are holy.

Those I have not yet met are holy.

I am holy.

Throughout this summer, my spirit had come to understand that all human beings are sacred tabernacles inhabited
by the Light, making me a part of all others and they of me. If
all humans are parts of the same Light, then acting out against
another, not only threatens one's own well being, but is ultimately an act against that Light. By honoring the divinity
in each other and appreciating the many alternative visions of
each human being to determine how best to live his or her life,
we could revolutionize and heal our world, I thought. *All hu-*
man beings are living tabernacles of the same Light, filled with its
grace, I repeated over and over again in my mind. I must strive
to never forget this most profound metaphysical lesson grasped
during my summer wanderings.

I found joy in the notion that the Spirit had given me sacred roots from which I could grow my life, while at the same
time giving me independent wings to determine how high I
might fly.

I suggested to Phil that, as he drove, it would help to pass
the time, if I read Campbell's book, *An Open Life*, aloud to
him. He agreed.

Thirty pages into the book, my mind felt as if it were
exploding. "Phil," I said, "an incredible thing is happening.
It's as if a book is writing itself inside my head. I thought the

sequence of books I read this summer was random, but my mind is arranging them into a logical outline for the book I intend to write. This is incredible; it's as if the books I read this summer were leading me where I needed to go. The Campbell book must have opened some mental floodgate. Amazing!" I grabbed a pen and inside the back cover of Campbell's book, I frantically scrawled concepts and book titles that had burst into my consciousness. An outline for a book and a synopsis of my summer's spiritual quest followed.

I recalled Campbell's words, "If you have the courage to follow your bliss, the thing that really gets you deep in the gut and that you feel is your life, doors will open up." Doors were indeed standing wide open in my life. I had come to realize I did have the courage to follow my bliss, to continue the transforming metaphysical journey I had begun on Cape Cod. In my heart, I realized I had many more miles to travel. I felt exhilarated by that notion.

After capturing the emerging outline on the inside back cover of Campbell's book, I felt certain that I would write about my summer pilgrimage in search of self, for my own daughters and grandchildren so that they would have a sense of who I am and thus better understand themselves. And, if luck would have it, I might even touch the lives of those beyond family, in hopes that my reflections might stimulate others to find their voices, to reassure those over sixty that it can be the most productive and exhilarating period of their lives.

In his book, Campbell instructs that "to have something new, something old has to be broken." Misconceptions, misinformation, passionate beliefs that have limited our ability to see the Light, in ourselves as well as in all other creatures, must be dispelled if we are to see anew. I felt an overwhelming sense of gratitude to Joseph Campbell for confirming the course of my summer pilgrimage, for being yet another mentor on my journey.

Campbell defines "hell as a place where people cannot sufficiently yield their individual selves in order to touch their internal grace." I knew that the grace and wisdom, the honest open sharing expressed by the multiple authors during my marathon summer reading had revolutionized my world view. The power of the written word, from so many writer/humanists, in conjunction with my own journal writing, had healed my anguished soul.

My greatest wish for our wasteland world, where individuals define each other by money and power, is that collectively we will be able to hear our spiritual and intellectual heroes, who over many millenniums have spoken to us about our common consciousness and a singular Spirit God.

Campbell writes that when the German philosopher Schopenhauer was asked how an individual can set aside his own self-protection and move spontaneously to another's rescue, Schopenhauer replied, "Spontaneous compassion, a compassion driven by the belief that you and that other are one, and that the sense of separateness is simply a function of the way we experience things in space and time." Spontaneous compassion explains my proclivity to save rabbits. To move spontaneously to another creature's rescue is not a weakness, it is strength, a noble undertaking.

I felt a deep sense of peace as we crossed into Pennsylvania. I pledged to myself to keep within my heart a place where dreams can grow, to continue to challenge myself to engage truth, to forgive intruders, and to strive to lift myself and others up to new heights of humanity through love. Certainly, I had learned that the adversities of life are intended to make us better, to grow our capacity for "spontaneous compassion."

I reflected upon Campbell's reference to "'the mystery of transfiguration,' of a spiritual passage which when complete, amounts to a dying and rebirth. Of familiar life horizons having been outgrown and old concepts, ideals, and emotional patterns no longer fitting; and the realization that the time for the passing of a threshold is at hand."

I had crossed over that threshold. I was returning home changed and strengthened, determined to write about my healing and my transcendent journey with the hope that it might provide a modicum of comfort and perspective to someone else's journey.

"By honoring the divinity in each other
and appreciating the many alternative visions
of each human being to determine how best
to live their lives, we could revolutionize
and heal our world."

Janet Brady Calhoun

SUMMER READING LIST:

It is my hope, dear reader, that you will be nourished and enriched, as I had been, by the authors and titles that guided my spirit during my summer sojourn . . . insightful reading on your sacred journey.

1. *A Year By The Sea*, Joan Anderson, Broadway Books, a division of Random House, New York, N.Y., 1999. One woman's Cape Cod year of self-discovery.

2. *Everyday Sacred*, Sue Bender, A Woman's Journey Home, HarperCollins Publishers, Inc., New York, N.Y. 1995. A journey of self-actualization and spirituality.

3. *Healing Zen*, Ellen Birx, Ph.D, R.N., Penguin Putnam, New York, N.Y., 2004. Buddhist Wisdom on Compassion, Caring, and Caregiving—for Yourself and Others.

4. *A Woman's Book of Life*, Joan Borysenko, Ph.D, Penguin Putnam Inc., New York, N.Y., 1996. A woman's book of life: the biology, psychology, and spirituality of the feminine life cycle.

5. *My Mother, Myself,* Nancy Friday, DelacoRoute Press, New York, N.Y., 1977. Daughter's Search for Identity

6. *Gifts From The Sea,* Anne Morrow Lindbergh, Pantheon Books, New York, N.Y., 1955. Meditations on youth and age, love and marriage, solitude, peace, and contentment during a brief vacation by the sea.

7. *An Open Life,* John H. Mahrer and Dennis Briggs, editors, Larson Publications, New York, N.Y., 1989. Joseph Campbell conversation with Michael Toms regarding legends, literature, mythology and spirituality.

8. *Ghosts From The Nursery,* Robin Karr Morse and Meredith S. Wiley, The Atlantic Monthly Press, New York, N.Y., 1997. Impact of childhood. Tracing the roots of violence.

9. *People of the Lie,* M. Scott Peck, M.D., Simon and Schuster, New York, N.Y., 1983. The hope for healing human evil. Letting go of anger, expelling demons.

10. *The Road Less Traveled,* M. Scott Peck, M.D., Simon and Schuster, New York, N.Y., 1978. A new psychology of love, traditional values and spiritual growth.

11. *Passages,* Gail Sheehy, E.P. Dutton, New York, N.Y., 1976. A book about hardships and loss and moving inward.

12. *Necessary Losses,* Judith Viorst, Simon and Schuster, New York, N.Y., 1986.

Losses: of loved ones; of giving up myths and magical thinking; of being able to protect those we love; of religious faith; of family myths.

New Hope for Binge Eaters, Harrison G. Pope, M.D., and James I. Hudson, M.D., Harper & Row, New York, N.Y., 1984.

The book I refer to in *Rabbit Warrior* that identified the source of my daughter's struggle.

ABOUT THE AUTHOR

JANET BRADY CALHOUN graduated cum laude from Franklin and Marshall College, Lancaster, Pennsylvania, at age fifty. She went on to become the first woman president of Lancaster City Council, the Lancaster County co-chair of Congressman Tom Ridge's successful gubernatorial campaign, and the Executive Director of Pennsylvania's First Lady's signature project. Janet completed her government service as Special Assistant to the Secretary of Human Services.

Janet spent five years writing her memoir and another five years deciding whether or not to "stand naked" in public by publishing her memoir. In the hope that one revelatory journey might add perspectives that soften the journeys of others, "standing naked" won out.

Janet resides in Lancaster, Pennsylvania, with her husband Phil, surrounded by her beloved children and grandchildren.

You may visit with the author at her blog or contact her via email.

janet@rabbitwarrior.com
www.rabbitwarrior.com